D0849803

THE WATCH ON THE RHINE

THE WATCH ON THE RHINE

The Military Occupation of the Rhineland, 1918–1930

Margaret Pawley

Published in 2007 by I.B.Tauris & Co Ltd
6 Salem Road, London W2 4BU
175 Fifth Avenue, New York NY 10010
www.ibtauris.com

In the United States of America and Canada distributed by Palgrave Macmillan
a division of St Martin's Press, 175 Fifth Avenue, New York NY 10010

Copyright © Margaret Pawley, 2007

The right of Margaret Pawley to be identified as the author of this work has been asserted by the author in accordance with the Copyright, Design and Patents Act 1988.

All rights reserved. Except for brief quotations in a review, this book, or any part thereof, may not be reproduced, stored in or introduced into a retrieval system, or transmitted, in any form or by any means, electronic, mechanical, photocopying, recording or otherwise, without the prior written permission of the publisher.

ISBN: 978 1 84511 457 2

A full CIP record for this book is available from the British Library
A full CIP record is available from the Library of Congress

Library of Congress Catalog Card Number: available

Printed and bound in India by Replika Press Pvt. Ltd
From camera-ready copy typeset by Oxford Publishing Services, Oxford

For my sister Pamela who shared my Rhineland childhood.

CONTENTS

LIST OF ILLUSTRATIONS

All photos are from the author's collection unless stated otherwise.

MAP OF THE RHINELAND OCCUPATION ZONES

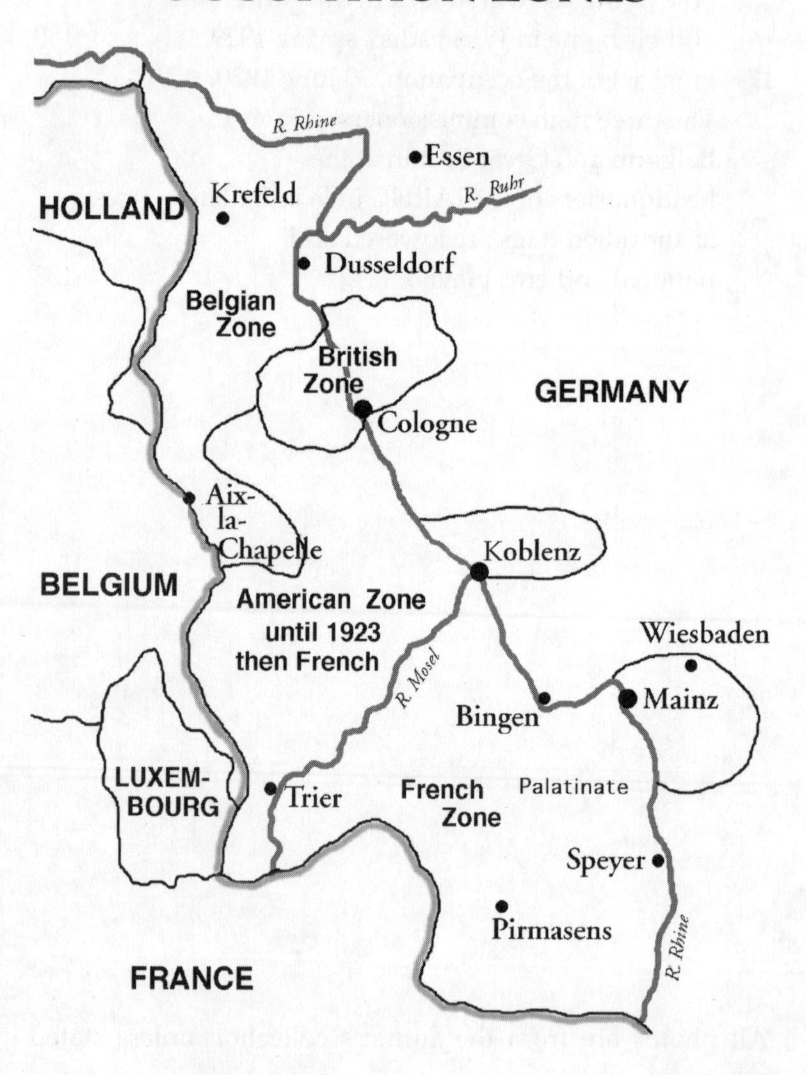

ACRONYMS AND ABBREVIATIONS

ACD	Army Chaplains' Department
AFG	American Forces in Germany
Bt	baronet
CB	Companion of the (Order of the) Bath
CMG	Companion of the Order of St Michael and St George
DSO	Distinguished Service Order
DVP	*Deutsche Volkspartei* (German People's Party)
GCB	(Knight *or* Dame) Grand Cross of the Order of the Bath
GCMG	(Knight *or* Dame) Grand Cross of the Order of St Michael and St George
GHQ	general headquarters
GOC	General Officer Commanding
HM	His Majesty's
HQ	headquarters
IARHC	Inter-Allied Rhineland High Commission

IMCC	International Military Commission of Control
KBE	Knight Commander of the Order of the British Empire
KCB	Knight Commander of the Bath (British military award)
KCMG	Knight Commander of St Michael and St George
KCVO	Knight Commander of the Royal Victorian Order
LVO	Lieutenant of the Royal Victorian Order
MICUM	Mission interalliée de Contrôle des Usines et des Mines
NCO	non-commissioned officer
NSDAP	National Sozialistche Deutsche Arbeiterpartei
OBE	Officer of the Order of the British Empire
RA	Royal Artillery
RE	Royal Engineers
RFA	Royal Fleet Auxiliary
SA	*Sturm Abteilung* (Storm Troopers)
SOE	Special Operations Executive
SPD	*Sozialdemokratische Partei Deutschlands* (Social Democratic Party of Germany)
WD	War Department
YMCA	Young Men's Christian Association

GLOSSARY

blutbad	bloodbath
Bürgermeister	mayor
Deutscher Tag	German Day
Deutsche Volkspartei	German People's Party
Einwohnerwehr	volunteer force of civil guards
Frei Corps	unattached force
Fürsorgstelle	consultation
Kreis	area
Oberbürgermeister	senior mayor
Oberregierungsrat	senior administrative adviser
Oberpfarrer	senior minister
Oberpräsidium	former headquarters of the Rhineland Province
poilu	informal term for a French infantryman
Polizeidirektor	chief of police
putsch	a revolutionary attempt
Rathaus	town hall
Realschule	modern secondary school
Regierung	government

Regierungspräsident	president of the executive council
Reichsbanner	banner of the realm
Reichsparteitag	party rally
Reichstag	Parliament
Reichswehr	a new German army
Reitervereine	cavalry show riders
Rentenbank	annuity bank
Rentenbriefe	annuity certificates
Rentenmark	currency issued in 1923 to stop hyperinflation
Rheinanlagen	a promenade in Koblenz
Sicherheitspolizei	security police
Stahlhelm	steel helmet (a counter-revolutionary veterans' organization)
Sturmabteilungen	Storm Troopers
tirailleurs	sharpshooters
Volksvereinigung	People's Alliance
Windjack	windproof jacket or jerkin

ACKNOWLEDGEMENTS

My thanks are due to many people. First to librarians who have painstakingly supplied me with books and material not readily available: at the Bodleian, my college library (St Anne's at Oxford); the British Library; the National Archives at Kew; the Army Museum Library; the Archive department of the Imperial War Museum; the Intelligence Corps Museum; and the Wye branch of the Kent County Library.

I wish to thank by name certain individuals who have been helpful. They include Dr David Williamson; Dr Roderick Bailey; Professsor Richard Holmes; the late Lieutenant-Colonel Tony Williams; Lieutenant-Colonel N. C. F. Weekes; Professor M. R. D. Foot; and Mr Pete Cleveland, who has provided me with information from the United States of America. My greatest debt is to Mrs Maureen de Saxe who, since publishers no longer welcome typewritten manuscripts, not only lent me her computer but, moreover, with considerable patience, taught me to use it, and helped me with the formatting.

Among the prohibitions laid upon the German population by the Allied occupying forces in the Rhineland in the 1920s, was the singing of militaristic songs; chief, of course, *Deutschland, Deutschland über alles,* the national anthem. The band of a riverside café dared one evening, in the presence of a group of British officers, to play the patriotic piece *Die Wacht am Rhein* (The Watch on the Rhine), a provocative reminder of nineteenth-century German history. The company present waited to see how the British officers would react. The officers rose to their feet, stood to attention and, on receiving thanks for this conceived courtesy, they replied '*We* are the Watch on the Rhine'.

INTRODUCTION

After four years of bitter trench warfare, the First World War came to a sudden conclusion at the instigation of the German High Command. It acknowledged defeat on 18 September 1918, an event that continued to be bitterly resented by the German nation as a whole, which regarded it as a 'stab in the back'.

While armistice terms were being prepared, and finally became operative on 11 November 1918, Marshal Foch, the Allied commander-in-chief, pressed for the Rhine to represent the new border of Germany. Refusal by Great Britain and America led to an alternative: the left bank of the Rhine and three bridgeheads at Cologne, Koblenz and Mainz, 30 kilometres deep, should be occupied by a joint Allied force as a guarantee for the payment of reparations in the future. No suggestions for the occupation of enemy territory had been made earlier, unlike the Second World War where elaborate plans were drafted during the course of hostilities. Sir Douglas Haig, commander of the British Expeditionary Force and Lloyd George, prime minister, were opposed to occupation and in particular by joint forces. Eventually, with American help, they won their case for the four Allied armies, French, Belgian, American and British, to occupy their own zones. The French agreed so long as the occupation should last 15 years – zones to be relinquished after five, ten, and then fifteen years' tenure.

In the meantime, the defeated German army made its way gradually from the Western front back to the Fatherland. It marched at the rate of about 20 miles in 24 hours, mainly at night, when French and Belgian citizens were asleep. Passing through Cologne, the German troops were treated as if they had been conquerors, but the triumph was short-lived because they needed to leave the bridgehead immediately while preparations were made for the arrival of the victors.

Following the cessation of hostilities on 11 November 1918, Foch declared a 'breathing space' of six days when only the German army was permitted to move. It was, therefore, not until 17 November that detachments of the British Second Army, under the command of General Sir Herbert Plumer,[1] became the vanguard of an occupation force (together with some units of the French army) and left Belgium for Germany. The Second Army comprised 11 infantry divisions (organized into four corps), and a cavalry division; 18 squadrons of the Royal Air Force were deployed in support. One of the corps was Canadian and there were small Imperial contributions from New Zealand, Newfoundland, Australia and South Africa. The total strength was nearly 275,000 officers and men. Great Britain had been allocated the zone and bridgehead based upon, and surrounding, Cologne. The French zone in the

1. Sir Herbert Plumer with Field Marshal Sir Douglas Haig and General Sir Herbert Lawrence, at General HQ Western Front, 1917.

south included the bridgehead at Mainz, the Palatinate, Rhenish Hesse and the Prussian Rhineland up to the Mosel.

The Belgians were allotted a small strip of land running from Aachen (Aix-la-Chapelle) to the Dutch border; the United States received the bridgehead at Koblenz and its hinterland. Belgian detachments set off for their zone around Aachen; Americans moved through the Eifel towards their zone round Koblenz and French troops under General Mangin advanced on Mainz, the centre of their area. The weather was extremely cold with frozen roads and hoar frost on the trees. Sir Douglas Haig fiercely resisted Foch's suggestion that some French divisions should be placed in the lead among British troops.

The British Second Army reached the German frontier on 30 November 1918, in preparation for crossing on 1 December and to reach the Rhine on 8 December. But no supply trains arrived for two days; the march needed to be halted and the troops billeted locally.

Led by the first cavalry division, the infantry moved into the outskirts of Cologne on 6 and 7 December. According to the armistice terms the Allies were not to cross the Rhine until 13 December. General Plumer wrote on the 12th.

> The weather was not very kind to us today, but it might have been worse and though it did come on to rain it did not begin until nearly all the troops had passed. I admit I was thrilled. The 2nd and 9th Cavalry Brigades marched through Cologne across the Rhine this morning. … I stood at the entrance of the Hohenzollen Bridge … and at 10 o'clock the Union Jack was unfurled and the troops commenced to cross. The band of the Blues played them

> past, men and horses looked splendid. ... Tomorrow the Infantry go across.[2]

The peace conference, which began in Paris at Versailles in January 1919, produced a treaty that the Germans agreed to sign after a tense period when the possibility of them not doing so was ever present. The tensions increased upon the desire of France to detach the Rhineland from Germany and create an independent province under French patronage and control. At the same time as the signing of the peace treaty took place on 28 June 1919, a supplementary document, entitled the Rhineland Agreement, set up a civilian body called the Inter-Allied Rhineland High Commission (IARHC) to oversee the military regime in the occupied zones and to take charge of economic matters. This system of setting up a civilian organization as the supreme authority during the military occupation of a conquered country was without precedent. It went some way towards creating machinery for consultation between the occupying powers and the local Rhineland authorities who retained their civil administration under German law and subject to a central German government. The French, British and Belgian high commissioners were to be appointed with their staffs. Ordinances would be drafted at regular meetings of the high commission for implementation by military and civilian bodies. The early days of the occupation were dogged by the determination of the French government and army leaders, as well as a small group of Germans, to separate the Rhineland from the rest of Germany.

My father, James Herbertson,[3] joined the Honourable

Artillery Company on 4 August 1914 and sailed for France on the *Westmeath* on 24 September. Once in the trenches his fluency in French and German became apparent. Several years in his youth had been spent on the continent and at Oxford he had read modern languages. He was commissioned as an intelligence officer, largely employed in the interrogation of German prisoners immediately on capture; he was also credited with crawling into no-man's land to overhear German conversations before a push. After some months with a French and an Australian unit, he joined the staff of General Sir Henry Rawlinson's Fourth Army at Namur, where the armistice found him. During February 1919 he was posted to Cologne.

By the spring of 1920, with the ratification of the peace treaty, plans for the establishment of the IARHC began to be made. (In reality it only became 'High' Commission after ratification.) The decision was taken that it should be based in Koblenz in the American zone. Sir Harold Stuart became high commissioner for Britain and James Herbertson was appointed his political officer. In July 1919 he came to England to be married; in August he returned from his honeymoon. His wife followed and they took up residence in Koblenz. They were to remain in Germany until June 1930, when Herbertson, having assumed the mantle of British high commissioner in the Rhineland, was the last official to leave the formerly occupied country.

One of Herbertson's duties as political officer was to compile annual reports for the British high commission on politics, and on economic and social events in the occupied zones. Earlier, in Cologne, the military governor, Sir Sidney Clive, had written of him:

2. James Herbertson interrogating a German prisoner in the Ypres salient 1916.

> He has been in charge of the section dealing with the political intelligence and control of political parties in the British Zone. The leading men of all these parties, Clerical, Independent, Socialist, Rhineland Republican etc. have acquired a habit of coming voluntarily to see him to explain their aims and plans in the frankest manner and to keep him informed of new developments.

These British high commission annual reports went to the Foreign Office and eventually found their way to the

National Archives; it is from there that they have been rescued for the purposes of the present work. They give an overview of the occupation of the Rhineland from its earliest days, in particular of the circumstances of the premature departure of the Allied forces and a forecast of consequent problems.

With the recent landing in Iraq by armies of several nations, the whole matter of occupation of foreign lands comes once more into focus. The occupation of the Rhineland in the 1920s is just within living memory. A recent radio programme by Professor Richard Holmes, entitled 'The Army of the Rhine', recorded the voices of some very old soldiers. Moreover, Monsieur Charles Wagemans of Ghent, son of a member of the Belgian high commission, and Valéry Giscard d'Estaing (later president of France), who was born in Koblenz and was the son of the French high commissioner's finance officer, are both still alive. The military occupation of the Rhineland by the victorious Allies after the First World War formed the background of my own childhood. I shall write of its beginning to its end.

I was born in the American Military Hospital on the left bank of the Rhine at Koblenz, then under the occupation of the army of the United States. My mother, from her window at the hospital, could see high up on the other side of the river the fortress of Ehrenbreitstein on which flew the American flag 'Old Glory'. A year later it was replaced by the French *Tricolor*. The pain caused to the German nation by the annexation of one of Germany's most important Rhine castles, and indeed occupation of the Rhineland as a whole, was very severe. The river was

3. The fortress of Ehrenbreitstein overlooking the Rhine at Koblenz, shown flying the French tricolor.

more than a major waterway; it was a symbol of national identity. German literature, myths and history extolled the majesty of the Rhine. It was to be expected that German patriots, as well as scoundrels, should struggle to lift the occupation, and were eventually successful in reducing the period of tenure originally set. These longings for freedom and independence were comprehensible. My own memories of the Rhineland and our lives there (when I never considered myself other than British) remain very vivid.

Important issues for the Allies to face, which dragged on for much of the occupation, were reparations and German disarmament. Under the Treaty of Versailles 'reparations' were interpreted as meaning that 'Germany should undertake to make compensation for all damage done to civilian populations of the Allies and their property by the aggression of Germany by land, by sea and in the air.'

Germany's failure to make these payments led the allies into various strategies, including, in the case of the French, having their troops occupy the Ruhr.

Later international undertakings took place under the Dawes Plan, the Young Plan and the Treaty of Locarno, to attempt to solve this problem. The clauses on German disarmament drawn up by the treaty were designed 'to prevent the danger of further aggression by Germany'. The continuation of the occupation was to guarantee the fulfilment of these clauses.

An example of forfeit, in respect of the lifting of the occupation of zone one (based on Cologne), came in January 1925 when Cologne continued to be occupied – until 1926 – because 'Germany had not sufficiently disarmed at the present moment to prevent her going to war with a civilized power'. The clause of the Treaty of Versailles that was not then of immediate significance was that of the perpetual demilitarization of the Rhineland. In 1936 its breach caused considerable international concern and the threat of a possible outbreak of war.

As I enjoyed my happy childhood in that part of Germany occupied by the Allies, black clouds were gathering over the same territory. Almost all the British high commission reports (drafted by my father) mentioned the existence of secret, and not-so-secret, societies that were being formed in parts of the Rhineland. Among the chief of them was the National Sozialistche Deutsche Arbeiterpartei or NSDAP (later known as the Nazi Party) and other groups with a militaristic outlook. They will be described in the chapters that follow. Long after the occupation, an intelligence officer[4] wrote of his experience with the British Army of the Rhine, of the Rhineland as one of the main centres of activity and propaganda of the emerging Nazi Party and of the visits there of Goebbels and Goering. He also described the small, and dwindling, size of the intelligence staff appointed in the Rhineland army and the limited importance given in British government circles to the information forwarded on Nazism and its dangers. As a former intelligence officer in SOE during the Second World War,[5] I regret this shortsightedness and its deadly and widespread consequences.

On Saturday 7 March 1936 Hitler announced to the assembled *Reichstag* that German troops were at that moment entering the Rhineland, demilitarized by the Treaty of Versailles. As he awaited the response of the signatories of that treaty, France and Great Britain, to this violation, he acknowledged later 'The forty-eight hours after the march into the Rhineland were the most nerve-wracking of my life.'[6] His move to end the demilitarized zone was not unexpected; it was seen only as a matter of time before Germany took this step to re-establish sovereignty over the Rhine area. There were two imponderables. First, when would this happen? In the event, only on 2 March did Hitler make the decision to give the order for the advance of troops, and with a force much smaller than could have been assembled by the French. Second, how would Great Britain and France react? After consultation the Allies decided to do nothing.

The code name given by the Germans to the plan for the military reoccupation of the Rhineland was SCHULUNG ('training' in English). Whether or not deliberate terminology, it was as a 'practice run' a warning of future moves to come – into Austria in March 1938; into Czechoslovakia in March 1939 and Poland in September of the same year. With a great deal of hindsight, the Earl of Avon, who as Anthony Eden was foreign secretary in 1936, wrote later in 1962: 'A militant dictator's capacity for aggrandisement is only limited by the physical checks imposed upon him. Hitler was not challenged until his power had been swollen by a succession of triumphs, and the price to be paid changed the history of our planet.'[7]

Chapter 1
CIVIL AFFAIRS (1918–20)

The end of the First World War found the morale of the German nation as a whole at a low ebb. Defeat was a severe blow, especially since, until the summer of 1918, the German army appeared to be winning. Social and economic unrest reached revolutionary levels. Spurred on by the spread of communism from Russia as a result of its revolution of 1917, mutiny among sailors in the dockyards of Kiel, strikes among factory workers led to the establishment of soldiers' and workers' councils on a soviet pattern; there was one such in Cologne. Demands were made to control the supply of foodstuffs.

Shortages were felt particularly strongly in the Rhineland because of the British blockade of ports, which continued until the peace treaty was signed and which the Belgian railways' poor communications exacerbated. Local horticultural production was low because of the high proportion of manpower that had been absorbed into the army. Important as it was to feed the population, the greatest problem of the months immediately following November 1918 was the restoration of law and order. The Rhineland was less beset by violent forces than Berlin, but Bolsheviks, members of the Red Army (revolutionaries loyal to the teachings of Marx and Engels), made their appearance, together with local dissidents.

The need for a new constitution followed the forced resignation and exile of the Kaiser and the end of monarchy in Germany. Elections to the National Assembly took place on 19 January 1919; for the first time women over 20 years of age received the vote (in advance of many of the other countries of Europe), which was by proportional representation. The delegates gathered on 9 February 1919 at Weimar, the birthplace of Goethe, as midwives of the new constitution and republic. Frederich Ebert[1] of the SPD (Social Democratic Party) was elected president on 11 February and a cabinet was formed of ministers from a balance of parties. Philipp Scheidermann, another Social Democrat, was elected chancellor.

The government of the new republic comprised two chambers: an upper chamber, the *Reichsrat*, and a lower chamber, the *Reichstag*. The commander of the German army, Field Marshal von Hindenburg[2] and General Erich Ludendorf,[3] had insisted that civilians should conduct the armistice negotiations; hence, Matthais Erzberger, a Centre Party *Reichstag* deputy, duly signed for Germany.

The ploy that the military should not be held as responsible for suing for peace, was eminently successful, and the Weimar Republic was to bear this burden for some time to come. The supposition that the peace terms outlined by Woodrow Wilson's 14 points would be more sympathetic towards Germany as against French and British demands, caused the German government on 4 October 1918 to approach the president of the United States with peace in mind. Woodrow Wilson took up the challenge and duly sailed for Europe to join the delegates to the peace conference – the first president to leave his country while in office. The two other main protagonists were Georges Clemenceau,[4] prime minister of France, and Lloyd George, prime minister of Great Britain.

Official meetings began in Paris on 12 January 1919 and the first point of discussion concerned the formation of a League of Nations as an association of countries working towards a peaceful international order. Describing Woodrow Wilson, Arthur Bryant said 'He shone with the lustre of a Messiah'. The weakness of his position, however, was that he, as a Democrat, did not reflect the views of the majority of the Senate who, as Republicans, in the last resort controlled American foreign policy.

Germany was kept ignorant of the proceedings of the peace conference until 7 May 1919 when a document of 44 articles was presented with a requirement that there were 14 days for it to be considered before the date of signing. Doubt was expressed about whether Germany would sign. In the British occupied zone, Lieutenant-Colonel I. H. Macdonell DSO of the 16th Highland Light Infantry in the Army of the Rhine, wrote to England on 26 June 1919: 'Have settled down at Haan, a village beyond Sölingen which is 25 miles east of Cologne, a frontier post next to the neutral zone. If the Huns don't sign, we shall be amongst the first troops to go into Germany.'[5] Here was corroboration 'on the ground' of instructions, from the Chief of the Imperial General Staff to Sir William Robertson, for British troops to advance into Germany, if necessary, to bring pressure on the Germans to sign the peace treaty.

With threats such as these, sign they did, on 28 June 1919 in the Palace of Versailles. However, the United States neither signed nor joined the League of Nations, despite Woodrow Wilson's mark on both. Most of the clauses of the treaty, like those that referred to the transfer of the German colonies, the fleet and certain territories that changed hands, such as Alsace-Lorraine, are not germane to the present enquiry and have no place here. There is a matter that is relevant that has already been mentioned: a supplementary paper, the Rhineland Agreement, which set out the nature of the occupation. The left bank of the Rhine and three bridgeheads were to be occupied by a quadrupartite military force, but with a supreme allied civilian authority – the Inter-Allied Rhineland High Commission, of which more later. The occupation was to last 15 years; zones were to be relinquished after five, ten and fifteen-year terms respectively, subject to conditions being satisfactorily carried out.

Clauses that referred to German disarmament and that reduced military and naval forces had their place in the peace treaty. While the German government had to pay for the occupation, the peace treaty had not fixed the total sum Germany had to pay as reparations for war damage and loss by the Allies. On 27 April 1921 an inter-allied commission, to be called the Reparations Commission, fixed

Germany's liability at 132,000 million gold marks - at that time £6,600,000. Reparations were to become the subject of lengthy and frequent consultations in the years to come. The word 'reparations' was used by my parents and their friends who came to our home in Koblenz when I was a child and I had no idea what it meant.

The question that requires a satisfactory explanation is why the successful allies took on the onerous task of occupying the Rhineland at all. The reasons have been simplified, particularly in the case of the USA and Great Britain. Obviously, it was in the interest of all the allies to oversee the achievement of German disarmament and the payment of reparations, but American sources[6] suggest that the matter of occupying Germany had a more complicated base. Naïve conclusions had attributed to Britain a fear of Russian ideologies and of Russia's huge population; an occupied Rhineland could act as a buffer state. In fact, it was fear of France's aspirations on the subject of the Rhine that affected both Britain and the USA most severely and caused the British, originally against occupation, to change their mind when the French attitude became obvious.[7]

Consultations between the allies about Germany's future had taken place in autumn 1918. Britain, represented by Field Marshal Haig, requested the surrender of the German fleet; Haig said that the territorial situation warranted asking only for what victors would permanently hold and was against allowing France to enter Germany 'to pay off old scores'. It became obvious that this was exactly what was in the minds of the French leaders.

At a conference held at the French HQ at Senlis on 25 October 1918 between Marshal Foch, Marshal Pétain, Field

Marshal Haig and the American General John J. Pershing, the Frenchmen argued in favour of an occupation of the left bank of the Rhine and certain strategic bridgeheads. Pershing thought that only the bridgeheads were necessary and Haig did not want an occupation at all, but he was defeated. On 1 November the British prime minister, Lloyd George, met Foch with the heads of government, and agreed to the marshal's proposals.

There can be no doubt that Foch saw occupation as the beginning of a process. Evidence exists[8] that he claimed on 27 November 1918 that the Rhine must be the western frontier of Germany and the eastern frontier of France. His alternative was to make the Rhineland a buffer state, separated from Germany and unarmed, while under French military control. British fears that occupation might lead to permanent arrangements, satisfactory to France, were to become amply realized with various separatist movements that were to come. As for the USA, Nelson writes that American occupation of the Rhineland 'prolonged through compromise and accident [was] perpetuated as much to restrain an ally [France] as to impress a former foe'.[9]

The birth of the Inter-Allied Rhineland High Commission, was by no means straightforward and had its curious features. While the Paris peace conference was hammering out the terms of the Treaty of Versailles, the Rhineland commission was charged with a brief to decide how that area was to be governed with the arrival of peace. Pierrepont B. Noyes, in his autobiography,[10] paints a vivid picture of some information to which he was privy. He was an American businessman and the director of the

Oneida Community, which had become a joint stock company manufacturing silverware. He experienced an interesting beginning; the Oneida Community had its origins in Wisconsin where its 350 members worked without wages for common support. It had made a radical experiment of eugenics: Noyes explained that a committee had planned the parentage of all but six of 54 children born in the community between 1869 and 1880, and that these children were not brought up by their parents. Noyes was one such child, born in 1870.

In April 1919, he found himself with a trunkful of cutlery in Paris and casually visited some acquaintances who were planning the Rhineland commission. Foch had set up Le Contrôl Générale de l'Administration des Territoires Rhénans (of which more later) as his advanced headquarters in Luxemburg. In pursuit of improving trade within the occupying territories and the west, France had also set up another commission in Luxemburg. The need for a strong civil body became apparent to those working on the peace conference in Paris. A proposition was made for a four-member Inter-Allied Rhineland Commission for which endorsement came on 21 April 1919. A search was in progress for an American commissioner. Noyes was persuaded that he was the man for the job. He writes that he joined the preliminary commission with some misgivings. He considered the British member to be a man of the highest integrity and ability; Sir Harold Stuart, who had spent 30 years in the Indian Civil Service, agreed with the American 'hands off as much as possible' theory for the occupation.

The commission's temporary headquarters were in

Luxemburg. The French commissioner, Monsieur Paul Tirard, reacted coolly to suggestions made by the two aforementioned and said that he must go for consultation to Paris. During a telephone call he apprised the others that a plan was being discussed that would make the Rhineland commission unnecessary. A group of allied generals under the influence of Foch had drafted a 'convention' that decreed that 'martial law with all its consequences' should remain for 15 years. It placed the control of the German police and 'the conduct of the occupation' in the hands of the French military commanders. Sir Harold and Noyes reacted violently. In a letter of 27 May 1919 Noyes sent a new plan of agreement concerning the occupation of the Rhineland[11] to President Woodrow Wilson in Paris. It changed the occupation from a military to a civilian one. The military should have a relatively passive role. This was 'to take control under martial law either in danger spots or throughout the territory whenever conditions seem to the Commission to make this necessary'. The President agreed and wrote : 'I am sincerely obliged to you for your helpful letter.'[12]

Walter A. McDougall corroborates in his book[13] that the drafting committee took as its basis for discussion not the suggestions of Tirard or those of Waterlow[14] or Foch, but a letter to President Wilson from the American representative on the Rhineland commission, Pierrepont Noyes. The civil commission was adopted.

Since the peace treaty came into force on 10 January 1920, the Rhineland commission became the Rhineland high commission from that date. It had already moved into the prestigious headquarters of the *Oberpräsidium* (former headquarters of the Rhineland Province) in Koblenz. 'It became the supreme representative of the Allied and Associated powers within the occupied territory and its ordinances. [It] ... received the force of law and the recognition as such by all the allied military authorities and by the German civil authorities.'

The IARHC ordinances were designed to protect allied military personnel with the German police responsible for general law and order, unless ordered otherwise. Internal daily matters of state, both central and local were the province of the German government. Allied officers known as *Kreis* (area) officers were posted as local representatives of the IARHC, as already described.

Monsieur Paul Tirard became French high commissioner and took possession of part of the *Oberpräsidium* as his home. He placed into its elaborate rooms (including a ballroom) furniture and tapestries from Paris, to make it commensurate with his status as president of the high commission.

Sir Harold Stuart became British high commissioner, and it was in his department that my father held the post of political officer. By this time my parents had already moved into a flat in the Rheinzoll Strasse in Koblenz. Baron Rolin Jacquemyns, who had been professor of history at the University of Brussels, became high commissioner for Belgium. He took little part in procedures, except to vote, usually with Tirard. At the request of the German government, the allied governments, with some hesitation, allowed Herr von Starck to join the high commission as a co-opted non-voting member: he did not prove himself able to carry out his responsibilities

4. The *Oberpräsidium* at Koblenz, headquarters of the Inter-Allied Rhineland High Commission (IARHC).

adequately and resigned on 30 May 1921. Prince Hatzfeldt-Wildenburg took his place.

To celebrate the ratification of the peace treaty, Tirard gave a grand jubilatory dinner to which all members of the high commission were invited. Since the United States had not ratified, Noyes and General Allen, commander of the American forces, were placed, so Noyes reported sadly, 'below the salt' at the dinner table.[15] Noyes remained American commissioner (not high commissioner) with no vote, a fact that would rebound badly for the British high commissioner who was almost always outvoted by France and Belgium. Noyes records that he enjoyed his work during his 14 months in the Rhineland, but they were 'fighting months. The fights were often bitter and I did not win all of them.'[16] In June 1920 he decided to return to the United States. There is little doubt that he was required to do so by the State Department. General Allen assumed Noyes's duties, with Colonel Stone as his representative at the sittings of the high commission.

The elections of June 1920 resulted in a disastrous defeat for the Social Democratic Party (SPD) and the Democrats. A centre-right government was formed under the elderly Constantin Fehrenbach. A move to the right was perceived and described by the British high commission's reports for 1920:

> The amalgamation of the greater part of the Independent Socialists with the Communists into one solid party, was causing uneasiness among groups on the Right and was to an extent the cause of a general effort on their part to strengthen their position in the country. The attitude of German officials to members of the occupation had stiffened. The parties of the Right had become more nationalistic and showed themselves anxious to increase their strength and popularity until a purely Right government could come into power with a working majority.

These were remarkably prophetic words. Although there was so far no mention of the NSDAP or Nazi party, it was not long in coming.

Chapter 2
MILITARY AFFAIRS (1918–22)

The British zone (1918–20)

The British Second Army entered Cologne in the early days of December 1918 in almost incessant rain and gazed upon by a large silent crowd. Until the Rhineland settlement became known and approved and the peace treaty ratified on 10 January 1920, the occupation was purely military: relations with the population were carried out by military governors under the direction of the military commander. The first of the military governors of Cologne was General Sir Charles Fergusson Bt; General Sir Herbert Plumer (later Field Marshal Lord Plumer of Messines) commanded the British Second Army, later in January 1919 renamed the British Army of the Rhine.

Plumer had an impeccable record as a leader in the field. He had served in South Africa, in the Matabele campaign, and distinguished himself in several significant engagements during the First World War; from one of these, the battle for the Messines Ridge, he took his title when he became a peer. He was born in 1857, was short in stature and delicate of build with a bald head, large white moustache and rosy cheeks. His strength of character was paramount. His biographer, General Sir Charles Harington, wrote of their long association:

> his earnest and loyal devotion to duty throughout all his service [which] in his last years was to make him an Army Commander, beloved and trusted by all who were privileged to serve under him.
>
> His career was founded on being a good regimental soldier. In that capacity he learnt the feelings of a soldier which he never forgot. He never pretended to be a man with what may be termed a brilliant brain or genius in any way. He just went through life doing everything thoroughly. Every action of his was based on common sense.[1]

This trait was shown in Plumer's attitude to the problems he found in Cologne. On arrival he wrote to his wife:

> It is a great honour to be the Army of Occupation, but it carries a good many penalties with it. I can see it will not be a bed of roses by any means. It has turned out a dreadfully wet day and all our troops on the march are getting wet through. One of the trains of supplies has broken down again, and the 1st Canadian Division will have to halt again

tomorrow. All very tiresome. However, the war is over and men are not being killed.

Plumer's difficulties were certainly considerable, both on the civil and military side. Among the German population there was much unrest. Anarchy and looting had been exacerbated by the presence of Spartacists (Bolsheviks) and general shortages. The soviet-style councils affected German local government. Konrad Adenauer, *Oberbürgermeister* of Cologne and, after the Second World War, chancellor of Germany, was handed a list of rules and regulations that were being imposed by the military authorities. On 12 December he received a visit from the military governor who outlined the projected occupation policy. Some of the details were fierce.

In a 7.00 p.m. curfew, civilians (who were all to be registered and their names identified by numbers) needed to stay indoors until morning. All telephones were disconnected and cars could only be used with special permission. Public meetings without leave were banned, censorship of letters, newspapers and cinemas was maintained, and central European time was changed to that of Greenwich. The regulation most resented required German men to raise their hats to British officers in the street. It was soon rescinded, but in the meantime it soon became apparent that many went bareheaded, in spite of the cold weather.

Such were the conditions of unrest that the security afforded by the presence of the British troops and their regulations became more appreciated than resented. On 11 May 1919, General Sir Henry Jackson commanding the 2nd

Brigade Eastern Division, wrote home to England that 'The Boche people don't in the least seem to resent our being here. In fact, they are undoubtedly glad, as we are at any rate preferable to their own Bolsheviks.'[2]

Major W. J. Nicolson of the Royal Horse Artillery, who arrived in Cologne on 16 January 1919, was required to find billets for the men and accommodation, if possible under cover, for the horses. 'It is certain that the Germans' war propaganda had poisoned the minds of their people against us, so you can imagine my surprise when I set off billeting, to find everybody so cooperative and many offered unoccupied bedrooms.'[3]

Meanwhile, industrial strikes threatened factory production. Plumer took the drastic step of issuing a proclamation declaring strikes to be illegal and forbidden. It was pointed out that it was in the interests of the people that the industrial trouble raging in Germany should not spread to the occupied territory, for it would lead to misery and starvation. A British arbitration court was set up to deal with disputes and was generally well received.

With regard to the food shortages for civilians, Plumer took the step of sending a telegram to Lloyd George, the British prime minister, while the latter was attending the Council of Ten, which was meeting to discuss the size of the German army in the postwar period. Plumer asked for an immediate supply of food to be sent to the British occupied zone to counteract a future Bolshevik rising. He pointed out how bad it was for the British army to witness starving women and children. Although he did not say so, there were incidents of British soldiers sharing their rations. 'Unless they allow food for the Germans to come here there will be trouble and the Army will be a police force.'

The food supplies arrived. Trouble already existed among the British troops in the Cologne zone who were war weary and longing to go home. Plumer, in conjunction with the Secretary of State for War Winston Churchill, arranged in January 1919 for 1200 men each day, increased to 2400 from 21 January, to be repatriated to reduce the Rhine army to ten divisions. Young 18 year-old soldiers from Britain would fill the gaps left by some of the veterans. As far as possible, Plumer spread out his soldiers throughout his zone, which was smaller than the areas allocated to the armies of Belgium, the United States and France, and kept as few as possible in Cologne.

Plumer left the Rhineland command on 19 April 1919, to the sadness of many. He became governor of Malta during a time of difficulty and proved himself once more such an able administrator that he was offered the governor-generalship of Australia, which he was forced to decline through lack of funds. He became high commissioner of Palestine as an alternative. I have every reason to be grateful to his family. His daughter Eleanor became principal of an Oxford college and offered me a place (which I accepted) after the Second World War.

On 1 March 1919 King George V held a review in Hyde Park of several young soldier battalions brought in from stations outside London and who had been ordered to join the army of the Rhine. A few days after the parade, Winston Churchill, as Secretary of State for War, offered General Sir William Robertson Bt, GCB, GCMG, KCVO, DSO, the command of the Rhine army.[4]

The circumstances were appropriate, for General Robertson had enlisted as a young soldier and had achieved his present status through the ranks. In various capacities, he had experienced a colourful army career – as a lance corporal at Brighton, lance sergeant at the musketry course at Hythe, troop sergeant major in Ireland, a subaltern in India, a student at the staff college of which he later became commandant, on the headquarters staff in South Africa, head of the foreign intelligence section of the War Office, director of military training, to France with the British Expeditionary Force and eventually Chief of the Imperial General Staff.

He arrived in Cologne on 21 April 1919 when the British Army of the Rhine consisted of five army corps, each of two divisions, with a cavalry division and various other troops making a total strength of about 220,000 men. Demobilization was being speeded up, which resulted in a shortage of trained cooks and permanent commanding officers. The possibility of an advance into Germany (in spring 1919) was one for which forward plans needed to be made. On his frequent inspections of units, Robertson discovered that the training of the young soldiers left much to be desired; he encouraged efforts to be made to raise standards.

A number of distinguished visitors came to Cologne: they included the King and Queen of the Belgians, who arrived by plane, which was a fairly unusual method of travel at the time; the Duke of Connaught, Commander-in-Chief of the rifle brigade came in May and held a review of about 10,000 men. Lieutenant-General Hunter Liggett, then commanding the American army of occupation, was another visitor, as was General Pershing, the American commander-in-chief who presented Robertson with the American Distinguished Service Medal. General Allen, who succeeded General Liggett, came often, as did General Michel, commanding the Belgian army of occupation: colleagues charged with similar responsibilities frequently exchanged visits.

Marshal Foch, with General Weygand, appeared on 16 May. He had begun a tour down the Rhine from Strasburg: he was received with a salute on entering the British zone from the British naval flotilla. Marshal Joffre visited in September.

The army council, represented by the Secretary of State for War, the Chief of the Imperial General Staff and the Adjutant General came to see as much of the Rhine army as possible; also clubs and regimental institutes. With the reduction in the size of the army, the arrival of soldiers' wives (instigated by Robertson) and the removal of the readiness to advance into Germany, the British zone became a typical garrison; with the YMCA, schools, hospitals, leisure centres, sports field, theatres, cinemas and so on.

The American zone (1918–20)

The figures that are provided in Keith Nelson's *Victors Divided* show the number of Americans who took part in the advance to the Rhine and this gives a sense of proportion to the occupying force. Whereas there were more than two million soldiers in the American Expeditionary Force in France, and half that number engaged in combat, only around 240,000 men participated in the occupation of Germany. Since the Rhineland Allied Army numbered in the vicinity of 750,000, Americans formed rather less than one-third of the allied force.

On 7 November General John Joseph Pershing[5] established the United States Third Army, entrusting it to Major-General Joseph T. Dickman, a cavalryman who had commanded the third division, and later the fourth and first corps. As finally constituted, the Third Army included five regular army divisions, two National Guard divisions, and two national army divisions. The orders distributed to the fourth division set out what was expected of those occupying Germany.[6] 'We are to help build a new government to take the place of the one we have destroyed; we must feed those whom we have overcome; and we must do all this with infinite tact and patience, and a keen appreciation of the smart that still lies in the open wound of their pride.'

Several of these aspirations would come to pass. Marshal Foch and General Pershing also issued proclamations to the inhabitants of the areas that the Americans were about to occupy. On 17 November, the Third Army began its march to the Rhine and on 21 November it passed in review before General Pershing in the city of Luxemburg, where they rested for six days. Germany had occupied the Grand Duchy of Luxemburg during the war and there was apprehension about how the people would react to the arrival of the Americans. An agreement was made with the retreating German army that American advance guards should follow the former at a distance of ten kilometres: this was the first agreement of its kind with the Germans since hostilities ceased. It had been a very long walk, in some cases nearly 200 miles. Some 596 days had passed since the United States had declared war on Germany and now an American army had arrived at the German frontier. The objective was the zone, designed for occupation by United States troops, of 2500 square miles centred on the ancient city of Koblenz at the confluence of the Rhine and the River Mosel. Overlooking the town, high up on the opposite bank on a lofty crag, was the castle of Ehrenbreitstein; it was soon to be filled with American soldiers and surmounted by the flag of the United States. On 2 May 1919 General Hunter Liggett replaced General Dickman as commander-in-chief of the American army of occupation and, on 2 July, the third army was dissolved and the troops became known as the American Forces in Germany, or AFG.

One of the most significant features of this force was the establishment of its newspaper, the *Amaroc News,*[7] which appeared daily from 21 April 1919 (with the exception of 26 December) until the last American left the Rhineland. Its pages reveal the detailed life of US troops in the Koblenz area against the background of the German scene. A most important early entry was the appointment of the permanent commander-in-chief, Major-General Henry Tureman Allen, on 7 July 1919. A biography by Heath Twichell Jr[8] and General Allen's own two books[9] on the period mean that the episode of the American Rhineland occupation is well documented.

While General Pershing ascribed to Allen the qualities that 'made him exactly the right man for the job', Twichell's biography dares to be more analytical.

5. General Henry T. Allen, commander of the American forces in the Rhineland.

A complex and unusual man, possessing many seemingly contradictory qualities; a haughty aris-

> tocrat who never lost his boyish sense of fun; a toughened veteran of three wars who devoted himself to the welfare and protection of war-ravaged civilians each time the fighting ended; an urbane sophisticate who obviously relished 'collecting' many of the great men of the era as his friends, and a supremely ambitious military professional with a profound understanding of the democratic tradition of his country. He was much else besides; a scholar, a diplomat, an author and even a politician.

As the American occupation developed, many of these traits were revealed. In a personal letter to Allen,[10] Pershing offered advice on how to maintain 'harmonious relations with the Allies and particularly the French'. (Pershing had suffered from this quarter.)

Keith Nelson comments in the same vein. 'The great irony of the occupation was that rather than draw the Allies together, it drove them further apart. Behind the façade of Allied unity in the Rhineland, significant tensions were developing, particularly between the French and American armies.'[11]

According to Allen's Rhineland journal,[12] they were not slow in coming. Foch and Pershing had had an earlier brush in November 1918 over the distribution of troops in the areas under occupation, which had caused Allen to declare that it was time 'that the American forces for once act independently of the French'.

Allen's journal recorded, as it was to appear many times over, that the French were trying to dominate the Rhine and that he had refused to yield the fortress of Ehrenbreitstein to them. Meanwhile, relations with the German inhabitants continued to improve. The *Amaroc News* was to run a campaign to feed and clothe quantities of German children. Billeting US soldiers in private houses had a benign effect on both parties. On 16 September the prohibition against fraternization between American soldiers and German women was lifted. German–American marriages were the next step.

Allen's journal illustrates that he cultivated his Allied colleagues. On 8 August 1919, General Robertson, the British GOC, arrived in Koblenz to stay, accompanied by the Earl and Countess of Carnarvon. Allen commented: 'While General Robertson is a rough and gruff Britisher, his good sense, cordiality, hospitality, and consideration have always been much in evidence in our relations.' Allen later made a return visit to Cologne, to dine and attend a ball. The Allies treated each other with outward courtesy. 'The usual guard of honour was turned out and the men were spick and span as always. In personal neatness and in general in the school of the soldier, they are well ahead of us, and I might say of the other soldiers of Europe.'

It may have been the sight of this British contingent that caused Allen to comment on 23 August on the 'undersized, ill-shapen men' under his command, and that the United States army needed 'physical culture'. After another inspection, he realized that the troops 'had not yet learned to march properly at the rate of 130 steps to the minute'. Allen wanted more than a competent force of field soldiers. The AFG needed to shine as a ceremonial unit. The generals of the four occupying armies, as has been seen, spent a good deal of time visiting one another's zones; whether the visit was official or social, Allen was determined for his troops to rank with the best. He was himself in good physical shape; tall and extremely handsome, he played many sports in the Rhineland, including polo. His diary for 4 September 1919 read 'played eight chukkas'.

By September 1919, the American forces in Germany had been reduced from 110,000 to 11,000 men, many of whom had recently come from the United States. It was no doubt these newcomers whom Allen found in poor condition. He organized his men into two brigades, each with an infantry regiment and a machine-gun battalion. One brigade also had an artillery battalion and a cavalry detachment; the other included a company of engineers and various other services and supply units. The AFG began what amounted to a second cycle of basic training.

Gone was the old routine of a half-day for training and half-day for play. Passes and leaves suddenly became a reward to be earned instead of a right to be expected. The new schedule included an eight-hour day of marching, shooting and practice manoeuvres with inspections at weekends and alert drills at any hour of the day or night. In the days to come, Allen heard praise of his troops from American and Allied sources. When the wartime three-star General Bullard visited Koblenz, he remarked that his country's forces in Europe were 'the most highly-polished and burnished soldiers the United States had ever had'.

In November 1919, Allen directed that all officers were to attend German classes and alternate with riding lessons; in the same month, he went out with the hounds himself in heavy snow; he also encouraged American soldiers to attend the *Realschule* in Cologne 'to extend their mechanical and engineering knowledge'.

For Christmas 1919, a large Christmas tree was prepared at Andernach just down the Rhine from Koblenz, for children under eight. The rivers Rhine and Mosel were dangerously high (as was to be my own experience in 1928), and reached the foot of the sentry boxes on the *Rheinanlagen* outside Allen's official residence beside what had been the edge of the river. By 27 December, he recorded, the water was rising three-quarters of an inch per hour; basements and cellars were under water; by 30 December the electricity had stopped and a generator had been supplied. The Rhine was the highest since 1882.

Marshal Foch paid General Allen a visit (on 9 March) as did General Michel, commander-in-chief of the Belgian occupation army at Aix-la-Chapelle (Aachen). His place was taken by General Rouquoy who called on 8 June 1920. When Allen made a visit to Cologne, the Black Watch formed a guard of honour to receive the American general who wrote: 'These Highland uniforms are something marvelous [*sic*] in their gaudiness'. With the departure of Pierrepont Noyes from the high commission in May 1920, General Allen, as his replacement, commented in his diary that he felt it had been a mistake to put a military man on a civil commission pre-eminently created to moderate the actions of military chiefs in the Rhineland.

US chief of staff General Peyton C. March visited the American Forces in Germany in June 1920. In *Weissenthurm* he inspected all the US troops on the Rhine and his report stated that 'The Composite Regiment that paraded in

Washington had nothing on your men.' It would seem that Allen's training had paid off. It appears that my parents had been invited to this auspicious event, since a photograph of it lies in one of my mother's albums.

On 25 August 1919 General Allen visited three US soup kitchens in each of which 400 German children were being fed. One meal each day was given to 2400 children in Koblenz, and 7600 in the surrounding country, through the Hoover and Quaker food supply. No Allied army did more to help the inhabitants of its zone than the Americans. The back of Allen's marble tombstone in the Arlington National Cemetery overlooking Washington, bears a bronze plaque. It reveals a handsome man in uniform surrounded by children and a mother with their hands outstretched in supplication and gratitude. The inscription below bears the words 'In grateful commemoration of the noble service rendered to the suffering children of Germany, 1924.'

The Belgian zone (1918–22)

Although the four occupation armies were each to be affected by the internal politics of its own country, Belgium found itself in a more insecure position at home than either Britain or France. This affected its position abroad. The Belgian army of occupation had been allocated an area smaller than that allocated to France and without a bridgehead. Moreover, it had the smallest army, five divisions as opposed to twenty French divisions, ten British and eight American. After September 1919 and the signing of the peace treaty, these figures were reduced to nine French divisions; the British and Belgians had five and the Americans half a division. The result was a modification of the occupation of the Saar, which passed to the government of the League of Nations. (The Reparations Commission gave Belgium 550 million marks from Germany from its first billion marks, accepting the contention that the Saar mines constituted payment for French army claims.)

McDougall describes, with the following, Belgium's political scenario: 'A tenuous balance existed in postwar Belgium between the Catholic, Francophonic and bourgeoise [*sic*] elements and a coalition of socialists and Flemings. The latter groups opposed the use of force against Germany. The occupation of the Ruhr could spark a crisis threatening the existing small monarchy.'[13]

An interesting example of current political pressures can be seen during a session of the Inter-Allied Rhineland High Commission in 1920. Rather unusually, the Belgian high commissioner supported his American and British colleagues by voting against a French military move into Darmstadt and Frankfurt. The following day, his vote was in the opposite direction. Pierrepont Noyes[14] enquired into the reason for this change of heart and discovered that King Albert of the Belgians had been present in the chamber during the first, but not on the second, occasion.

The King and Queen of Belgium had become extremely popular during the course of the war and they were regarded as a symbol of Belgian resistance to the German invaders. This popularity followed the monarch during his visit to the Belgian army of occupation in Germany as early as January 1919. An anonymous article entitled

'L'Armée belge au Rhin' lies among the papers at the Imperial War Museum. It describes (in enthusiastic terms) this visit of the king to the Rhineland.

There was considerable surprise, so early in the occupation, at the arrival at the port of Düsseldorf 'of their smiling soldier King'. He went directly to the Belgian frontier post and observed the formalities imposed on the Germans for the crossing of the bridge. The Belgian soldiers present were all war veterans and they 'saluted their chief who had also been their comrade with warmth and deep emotion'. The king spoke, much as usual, with officers, NCOs and men, and he enquired about their needs. He subsequently returned to Brussels by air.

A problem felt exclusively by the Belgian army, in the absence of a bridgehead, was its close proximity to unoccupied Germany and areas of trouble, such as the Ruhr. The headquarters of the Belgian army was at Aix-la-Chapelle; its troops were stationed at Krefeld, a few miles from the border. Consequently, the *putsch* of March 1920 was felt more keenly by the Belgian army than any other.

Monsieur Charles Wagemans recalls his father's service with the Belgian cavalry at Krefeld, before his appointment to the staff of the Belgian high commissioner at Koblenz.

> Attempts to disarm some of the *Frei Corps*'[15] formations round Berlin to comply with the Treaty of Versailles and its military restrictions, helped to trigger off a right-wing military coup against the regime. Led by a Prussian official by the name of Kapp, government buildings in Berlin were occupied by a mixture of *Frei Corps* and regular

> units in the early hours of 13 March. The cabinet fled to Dresden and then to Stuttgart, but before departure appealed to Berlin workers to declare a general strike to abort the coup.

The coup collapsed and Wolfgang Kapp was unable to form a government. Though the general strike was called off, workers in some industries were anxious to continue their left-wing offensive. Red Army units in the Ruhr led workers' strikes of 50,000 strong. Elsewhere, there were uprisings, for example in Saxony, Bavaria and in the Ruhr, and more than 1000 workers were killed. In the Ruhr, which was very near the Belgian zone, the insurrection included use of some 'pieces of artillery'. When groups of communists penetrated the 'neutral' demilitarized area close to the Belgian frontier, they adopted 'a hostile attitude' towards Belgian attempts at reconciliation.

France responded on 6 April by occupying Frankfurt and Darmstadt against the wishes of the USA and Britain. At the 'pressing request' of the French government, Belgium 'rather regretfully' sent a token military detachment. The operation provoked violent anti-French demonstrations. In Frankfurt a section of black *tirailleurs*[16] opened fire and killed and wounded a number of Germans. Shortly afterwards, the Allies conferred at San Remo. The *Reichswehr*[17] was made to withdraw from the Ruhr and, on 18 May, contingents of the French army evacuated Frankfurt and Darmstadt. The action of the black *tirailleurs* was not, however, easily forgotten and will reappear.

The Belgian article goes on to explain the reaction to the

failure of German compliance with certain requirements of the peace treaty: disarmament, reparations and acceptance of 'war guilt', for reasons 'sometimes plausible, sometimes not'. In Belgium, as in France, and indeed in Germany, socialist leaders pursued a policy of conciliation and in favour of appeasement. These circumstances complicated the role of France and Belgium in Germany.

The financial default and the German ill will that France had seen in the last months of 1920, envisaged an occupation of the Ruhr. The beginning of March 1921 saw a German refusal to bow down to the financial requirements of the peace treaty. With the agreement of Belgium and Britain, France began the next operation; this was the military occupation of the bridgehead of towns and ports on the river, Düsseldorf, Duisberg and Ruhrort. On 8 March 1921, at daybreak, a French battalion entered Düsseldorf by the port of Oberkassel, while the other two French battalions were accompanied by the British contingent of a squadron of cavalry, a few tanks, five boats of the Rhineland flotilla and a squadron of planes. All were under the orders of a commandant of the Belgian occupation army. At the same time Franco–Belgian troops entered Duisberg and Ruhrort.

In this section the Allied troops were under the command of the Belgian General Beaurain. The three bridgeheads were considered 'territories in a state of siege' and not under the control of the Rhineland high commission. A customs barrier, considered under the guise of sanctions, was established, which was badly received by the local population and moreover was not effective. At Duisberg the expulsion of a high functionary produced an uprising before a Belgian general. Around 1500 Germans shouted and gesticulated; the police of the political and security branch made 30 arrests, the crowd continued to demonstrate and a Belgian officer needed assistance. An officer of the gendarmerie and ten soldiers on horseback chased the crowd. In fewer than ten minutes it had dispersed and order had been re-established; nothing remained other than 'capes and canes'. On 11 May, the Germans concluded the protest.

The Belgian zone of occupation was not itself secure. On 30 June 1922, a bomb exploded on a military train, killing ten Belgians and wounding forty others. The frontier between occupied and unoccupied Germany was closed for some days.

The British high commission report for 1921[18] describes the very strong feeling that had arisen in Belgian occupied territory because of the Belgian attitude to the Eupen and Malmédy plebiscite. The Treaty of Versailles had allotted the two areas to Belgium subject to a vote by the inhabitants that this was their will. The Germans had alleged that the populations of Eupen and Malmédy were being starved in an attempt to persuade them to choose Belgian overlordship. The two *Bürgermeister*, it was said, had been directed to cut off the food supply of any person who protested. A state of siege existed in Aix-la-Chapelle, the headquarters of the Belgian army; an appeal had been made to the high commission.

Paul Tirard's monumental volume on his experiences of the Rhineland, *La France sur le Rhin,* includes a few examples of Belgian participation, particularly when these covered subjects of wider relevance. He writes of visits by members of the German government to the occupied zone. Some German ministers, like Joseph Wirth and Gustav Stresemann, had always observed *'une attitude courtoise'*. This was not the case when Dr von Simons, the German foreign minister, went to British occupied Cologne with the chancellor, Constantin Fehrenbach, on 15 November 1920.

Von Simons delivered what was described as 'an unforeseen and violent anti-allied speech' before going on to Aix-la-Chapelle. There he made 'intolerable attacks' on the treaty relating to the incorporation by Belgium of the cantons of Eupen and Malmédy. When knowledge of these speeches came to the attention of the Allied high commissioners, they apprised their respective governments. It was recommended that advance notice of future visits by German ministers to occupied territory be given. Meanwhile, Dr von Simons and Chancellor Fehrenbach left Aix-la-Chapelle the same evening and returned to Berlin without crossing into the French zone.

The French zone (1918–22)

In Tirard's book,[19] which was written immediately after the evacuation of the Allied armies from the Rhineland in 1930, he described French aspirations following the cessation of hostilities in 1918. 'What did France demand? Not enlarged territories, not annexation, not even the satisfaction of *amour propre*, nothing but her security.'[20]

The Allied complaints, which were shrill and very frequent, that France was seeking to dominate the Rhineland, to divide the territory, to separate certain portions of it and to impose a regime that was sympathetic to France, failed to comprehend what lay at the base of these desires. France had been invaded by Germany not once but twice in living memory – in 1870 and then again in 1914. Intolerable damage had been done to the French countryside, towns and villages; French casualties had been enormous. The need for security for its borders in future was consequently great. Separatism in the Rhineland as an answer to this problem will be discussed in the following chapter.

In his book *Occupation*,[21] a journalist called Ferdinand Tuohy, who experienced this period in person, wrote about the French use of the concept of 'glory'. The need for *gloire* dominated their military history and current business. Tirard's long work is peppered with the term; in fact, page 457, which ends the book, concludes with these words: *'Je salue ses drapeaux qui rentrent en France, immaculés dans la gloire.'* Tuohy's book contains a conversation on the subject with Georges Clemenceau, when he was the prime minister of France, who observed: 'A thing I like about you English is that you don't give a thought to glory; we are mad about it'.[22]

France required reparation of a special and a monetary sort for the ignominies suffered in two wars; it also needed an assurance of security for the future. The behaviour of its generals and armies in the Rhineland gave evidence of the need for both. An early example lay in the movements and attitude of Marshal Foch. On the morning of the armistice, he issued an order of the day addressed to the officers and soldiers of the Allied Armies. 'Be proud,' he said, 'You have adorned your colours with immortal glory.'

On 26 November 1918, on his way towards establishing his headquarters as commander-in-chief in Germany, he stopped at Metz. This was a highly significant act because he had been a student in that city 47 years earlier, before it had been annexed by Germany, as indeed had the whole of Alsace-Lorraine, as a consequence of the Franco-Prussian war of 1870. If Foch's biographer is correct, it was during the Metz visit, with all its memories, that he addressed a letter to the French government on 27 November claiming that the Rhine should be the future western frontier of Germany and 'further that the victors must mount guard upon it in perpetuity'.

Foch, as already shown, established his headquarters first in Luxemburg and then at Kreuznach on the River Nahe, south of Bingen, thereby closer to the Rhine. Meanwhile, on 19 November units of the French army of occupation had begun the long trail to Mainz under the command of General Charles Mangin,[23] one of the most capable and fearless of the French generals. Other troops pressed on to Speyer under General Gérard's command.

France had been able to arrange to occupy a much larger zone of the Rhineland than any other ally, stretching as it did from the upper Mosel to Strasburg in Alsace, and with a far greater number of troops; 30 divisions of pale-blue clad soldiers poured into the Rhineland.

Examples have already been given of French incursions into unoccupied Germany; in the case of Darmstadt and Frankfurt on 6 April 1920, and Düsseldorf, Duisberg and Ruhrort in March 1921.

Failure on the part of Germany to pay what were considered adequate reparations provided the reasons. The

6. General Charles Mangin.

occupation of these cities was reasonably soon relinquished, but bitterness endured in the cases of what can only be regarded as lack of consideration to its ally on the part of France. The first were the attempts to place French troops within areas already filled by the troops of allies; this was not according to the original agreed pattern.

From the French point of view, although their area was large, it did not contain 'the political, commercial, financial and religious heart of the Rhineland, Cologne' and, in the autumn of 1919, a suggestion was made to Downing Street that the reduced British army of occupation might transfer its headquarters to the university town of Bonn, thus allowing Cologne to be placed under the control of French troops.

This proposal found no favour in London. Efforts were then made to secure a section of the British zone at Cologne for French soldiers; it was met in part. The quarrel between Marshal Foch and General Pershing increased in tempo and took on serious dimensions when the former tried to have French troops infiltrated into Koblenz. The attack (which has already been described) in Frankfurt in April 1920 on the rioting German population by the French army's black troops (who formed a section of the *tirailleurs*) exacerbated the second and more serious lack of consideration for the reputation of the Allied occupiers.

As a gift to German propaganda, it was exploited to the full, remained considerable, of long duration and news of it reached the United States. A report dispatched to the State Department indicated that during the period January 1919 to June 1920, the average number of Negro troops in the French army of the Rhine was 5200 men. The average number of French colonial troops composed of natives of Africa, not of pure Negro blood, including distinct peoples such as Arabs from Algeria and Morocco, and Negroids, was 20,000 men.

During the period of occupation from 1918 to 1 June 1920, the cases of extreme misbehaviour on the part of French black troops officially reported to the French military authorities had not been considered unduly large. The number of non-white troops, yellow and black, chiefly yellow, who remained in occupied territories (on 21 April 1921) was reported as 27,500.[24] It was a large number and can be regarded as provocative on the part of the French authorities and less than considerate towards their Allies, upon whom the reputation of a fellow army would inevitably rebound, particularly since the number had been increased during the past year. The matter had been grossly exaggerated in the German press.

The British high commissioner, Malcolm Arnold Robertson, had expressed his regret that, while there was no evidence that 'black' colonial troops committed outrages more frequently than other troops, there was no doubt that Germans felt their presence in such high numbers to be a humiliation, and that this was the main cause of the hostility felt towards the French. It was strange behaviour on the part of the French generals that, while trying on the one hand to ingratiate themselves to the German population through various economic means, they should have been unable to recognize that the German image of 'black' troops differed from their own.

Chapter 3
SEPARATISM IN THE RHINELAND (1918–24)

Since the articles of the Treaty of Versailles had dashed French hopes of creating, with the Rhineland, some form of permanent buffer state against Germany, other strategies had to be found to secure the safety of France. Paul Tirard, the French high commissioner, was to be the prime mover.

From the beginning of the occupation, intelligence from all French commands had filtered through to Paul Tirard of the existence of separatist movements in the Rhineland, though their motives were unclear. Tirard, in his turn, promoted the idea that the Rhineland population should be persuaded that its economic interests lay with the Allies. He wrote a *rapport* to this effect on 19 December 1918.[1] If markets could be provided by France, belief in the feasibility of succumbing to French pressure politically might be the result.

The same month, a meeting of 5000 Rhenish citizens had assembled in Cologne on 4 December to resolve whether the official representatives of the Rhenish and Westphalian people should proclaim the constitution of a self-governing republic within the German confederation. Two Centre (Catholic) party members spoke: Father Fastert and Dr Trimborn. Another meeting took place, also in Cologne, on the following day of 'The League for the Rhenish Freedom'. The speakers were members of different political parties, Professor Dr Eckert (Democrat), Dr Hoeber (Centrist) and Jean Meerfeld (Socialist); the assembly hailed 'the Rhenish Freedom'.

Dr Adam Dorten, a young lawyer from Wiesbaden, who was disinterested in law but enthusiastic about separatism, commented in his pamphlet on the event that, 'Instead of energetically forming the new state, this was an attempt to try to make all parties cooperate in the solution of the problem; a plan that was bound to fail.'[2]

The father of this 'utopian idea' had been the *Oberbürgermeister* (lord mayor) of Cologne, Konrad Adenauer, who took the lead. At the invitation of Adenauer, G. E. R. Gedye, *The Times* correspondent, visited Cologne. It looked to him 'as though Berlin and after it all unoccupied Germany, was foredoomed to Bolshevism'.[3] This gave impulse to a temporary movement for some measure of separation of the Rhineland from the rest of Germany. The official Centre Party newspaper *Die Kölnische Volkszeitung,* gave its support for such a partition. Committees were formed during December 1918 and leaders of the Democratic and Socialist parties (Falk, Meerfeld and Sollmann) gave their alliance. The Rhenish deputies who had just been elected for the National Assembly and the mayors of the Rhineland towns, were summoned to the City Hall of Cologne on 1 February 1919, in order (in the words of Dr Dorten) 'to proclaim the solemn foundation of the Rhenish Republic'.

Some of the delegates were in favour of an immediate proclamation, but under Adenauer's influence, a committee, with him as chairman, was charged with working out a plan for founding a west-German republic within the German confederation. Adenauer had spoken for three hours and 'had adopted a subtle tone'. His biographer[4] explains that Adenauer's attitude towards a Rhineland state 'fluctuated in inverse proportion to his perception of the French threat'. The committee formed on 1 February held its only meeting on 30 May and discussed conversations Adenauer had had with French military officials; there was no further outcome; he was later to deny having promoted separatism *per se*.

The separatist movement thereafter suffered a split; moderates followed the Adenauer-led Centre Party and, choosing to respect warnings from Berlin, they lay low. Separatist die-hards attached themselves to Dr Dorten and his colleagues. With respect to the 'French threat', Tirard's *Rapport* of 19 December 1918 received support in Paris. The French secretary-general, Monsieur Philippe Berthelot, endorsed the idea 'of gradual infiltration and support for autonomist tendencies',[5] and looked to economic as well as military measures and reparation guarantees, which could include French control of mines, forests and customs in the Rhineland. If 'the French worked quietly and stressed economics, the British would be unable to act'. But Tirard's 'softly, softly' approach was overtaken by French military initiatives.

Marshal Pétain issued directives to the generals on the Rhine and told them to communicate with Foch on the issue of separatism. Dorten and other separatists were given the opportunity to respond and make appropriate contact with local military commanders. The first general to do so was Gérard, commanding the 8th Army in the Palatinate. 'The inhabitants,' wrote Gérard, 'see in us an insurance against anarchy and guarantee of a better future. We must show them that separation from the Right Bank is in their material and idealistic interests.'[6] Gérard began to prepare his population for its independence with the provision of lessons in French and an exhibition of French art at Zweibrücken. When he learnt that there was a separatist movement 'rumbling locally',[7] he invited local notables to meet him in Landau on 31 March. He became acquainted with a separatist leader Dr Haas, a chemist, who had a few followers and who pronounced himself ready to lead a movement. The German authorities feared a coup; Haas was arrested; separatist action was put on hold.

Meanwhile, Dorten had been able to speak to General Mangin,[8] the commander of the French 10th Army in Mainz, who was as enthusiastic as Gérard was over the matter of separation of the Rhineland. Dorten had attempted unsuccessfully to have an interview with the American General Dickman in March; Mangin proved more sympathetic.

On 19 May, after speaking to Dorten and other separatists, Mangin approved of a scheme that would create a semi-independent republic engulfing the whole of the left bank of the Rhine. In order to prevent a violent reaction by his fellow Allied commanders, American, British and Belgian, on the night of 22 May 1919 he dispatched couriers to alert them of his action. General Liggett reported the scheme to Paris, with a good deal of irritation, where the news and a protest were relayed from General Pershing to Woodrow Wilson and Clemenceau, the French prime minister.

On the British side popular feeling against autonomy ran high. General Sir Sidney Clive, the military governor, also went to Paris. He saw Lloyd George who was temporarily in residence and who said he 'did not want to see Germany further weakened and the Rhineland broken away'. When approached by General Mangin's chief-of-staff about how the British would react to a separatist coup backed by the French, Clive replied 'We are here to keep order [and] that is what we shall do.'[9]

The British commanders on the Rhine were given to such laconic remarks. General Sir Thomas Morland, who had served in Nigeria commanding a force in a territory almost the size of France, succeeded General Robertson in March 1920. However, he developed tuberculosis and was forced to retire. He was succeeded on the Rhine by General Sir Alexander Godley, an Irishman who had earlier commanded the fourth corps there. With the spread of separatist activity in other towns of the Rhineland he reported, in answer to a worried telegram from the War Office, that there was 'no cause for anxiety in the British Zone'. The majority of the civil population 'were all for a quiet life'; trouble was only likely to come by armed bodies entering from outside: barricades had been erected and British troops were held in readiness for any attack.

Meetings of separatists were held at Aix-la-Chapelle, Mainz and Speyer where a proclamation was designed. The Cologne committee had transferred its rights to that of Aix-la-Chapelle and so had the committees of Bonn, Cleves, Krefeld, München Gladbach, Neuss and Trier. The Aix-la-Chapelle committee transferred all these full powers to Dr Dorten and charged him with proclaiming the Rhenish Republic on behalf of the Rhenish Committee and those of Hesse-Nassau and the Palatinate.

It was one thing to produce a proclamation, but another to find somewhere to proclaim it. The first attempt by separatists with French help was intended for Koblenz on 22 May, but the Americans withheld their consent. A second try on 29 May at Aix-la-Chapelle, was also foiled; when Dorten arrived, poised to make his proclamation, the Belgian army under General Augustin Michel prevented him from taking any action.

The proclamation needed to be made in the French zone; it took place on 1 June 1919 and was posted up, or published, simultaneously at Aix-la-Chapelle, Mainz and Speyer. Together with assurances of help to come in the establishment of peace, it was declared that 'An autonomous Rhenish Republic, a Republic of peace, is founded within the German Confederacy, it comprises Rhenish Prussia, the former Duchy of Nassau, Rhenish Hesse and the Palatinate. ... Koblenz will be the seat of government and of the Rhenish Assembly, the provisional Government has its temporary seat at Wiesbaden.' Dr Dorten dispatched telegrams outlining the declaration to the peace conference and occupying powers; to the German president, Frederich Ebert, and to the prime minister, Philipp Scheidermann.

The designs of the Rhenish Republic were stated as:

- To make the Rhenish people benefit by the universally recognized privilege of transacting their own business.
- To save from ruin and Bolshevism the healthy portion of the German people and to give the other portion an example of their loyalty and desire for peace
- To secure future peace by fighting the influence of the Prussian spirit in Germany.

Dorten and a handful of followers entered the government building in Wiesbaden on 1 June 1919 (assisted by Colonel Pinot, French liaison officer there). He announced himself as president of a new buffer state; posters appeared all over the town. A general strike was declared and for five days disorder reigned until the *putsch* was allowed to peter out. German police tried to arrest Dr Dorten, protected as he was by French troops. Later, Clemenceau recalled General Mangin and General Gérard to Paris. Their armies, the 10th at Mainz and the 8th at Landau, merged into the French Army of the Rhine under General Degoutte on 21 October 1919.

Harry E. Nadler[10] points out that the greatest failure of the French military and occupation authorities was their refusal to believe their own intelligence on the nature of the Rhenish movement and that it was not pro-French, but

7. General Degoutte, commander of the French army occupying the Rhineland.

anti-Bavarian and anti-Prussian. This failure of intelligence was, as suggested earlier, shared by the British in relation to the development of the Nazi movement.

Among British high commission papers are undated 'Notes on the present situation as regards the movement towards a Rhineland Republic in the Occupied Zone'. They can be abridged as follows:

Since the proclamation at Wiesbaden on l June of a

West Rhineland Republic under the presidency of Dr Dorten, considerable changes had taken place in the organization and progress of the movement. Although from Dr Dorten's point of view the attitude of Weimar necessitated immediate action, yet the moment chosen by him to proclaim the republic was singularly ill-chosen and very premature. The movement suffered at the time from the following weaknesses

- Three leaders had just paid a visit to General Mangin at which the General was said to have stated that France had absolutely no interest in a republic which was not independent of Germany. In consequence of the publication of this interview, many adherents of a West Rhineland Republic were estranged and a strong cry of infidelity to the Fatherland was raised against Dr Dorten and his followers.
- There was a great lack of cooperation between the leaders of the movement in Cologne, Mainz, Koblenz and Aix-la-Chapelle.
- The Rhinelanders were, as a whole, quite unprepared for such a declaration. The amount of propaganda and general political campaigning that had been carried out was absurdly insufficient.

The Rhineland Republic, under the presidency of Dr Dorten was generally regarded as a failure and soon lost even a place in the daily press. A considerable section of the population of the Rhineland held aloof from the movement because they disapproved of Dr Dorten's hasty action and foreseeing its failure. This section had been growing in strength. The current progress of the movement was based on the following points:

- Dr Dorten had made it clear in his pamphlet,[11] that he was working for a Republic within the German Empire.
- The National Assembly, by the passing of Article 18 of the Constitution, had admitted the principle of the creation of new states through self-determination. This disposes of the cry of high treason raised by Berlin against Dr Dorten and his followers.
- Resulting on a large 'all party' meeting at the beginning of August, an executive committee for the creation of a West German Republic had been established in Cologne. Their object was to begin a well-organized political campaign.

In consequence of these changes, the attitude of some political parties towards the establishment of a Republic had also undergone some transformation. The Independent Socialists who were formerly strong opponents of the proposal, had split into two camps; some had accepted the idea of a Republic; the Centre Party remained largely in favour.

The notes continued:

> In present circumstances it was impossible to form any accurate estimate of the real strength of the Rhineland Republican movement. A large number who were in favour feared, in consequence of the hostility reigning at Weimar, to declare themselves as open supporters. In view of the improvement in organization and propaganda, the movement might become of principal importance. It was possible that the municipal elections which were to be held in about six weeks would be fought out largely on this question.

The failure of the *putsch* of June did not discourage Dorten and his French supporters: 1920 was to be an eventful year. November 1919 had seen the formation of the *Volksvereinigung* (roughly translated as People's Alliance) to promote the Rhenish Republic movement. On 22 January 1920, at Boppard on the Rhine, Dorten held his first meeting. *Oberpfarrer* Kastert presided while Dorten had a modest place on the committee. In a resolution the *Volksvereinigung* announced that the declaration made by the Centre Party at its January congress corresponded in a remarkable fashion with the plans of the *Rheinische Volksvereinigung* for the new constitution of the German empire and the immediate splitting-up of Prussia as a necessary preliminary for the recovery of Germany.

The 'much disturbed' Centre Party retaliated and in a meeting on 3 February passed its own resolution opposing that of the *Volksvereinigung*. On 4 February all political parties in Cologne, with the exception of the Independent Socialists, signed a declaration that they would expel any of their members who belonged to or supported Dr Dorten's *Volksvereinigung*. The Socialists, although refusing to join the resolution, declared they were in favour of its message and would also expel any members of the *Volksvereinigung* from their ranks. When some Prussian ministers made an official visit to the Rhineland, Prime Minister Paul Hirsch issued a warning against the separatist movement.

The spectacular arrest in Wiesbaden of Dr Dorten by Frankfurt police on 24 July 1920 evoked inter-allied discord of no mean sort. The high commission informed the German commissioner that Dorten was to be returned to Wiesbaden, and this was done. At the time of the incident, Monsieur Tirard was temporarily absent in Paris and on his return, with feelings running high, he ordered the suspension of the *Regierungspräsident* and the *Polizeidirektor* of Wiesbaden; also the surrender to the French military courts of the Frankfurt police agents who had abducted Dorten, the driver of the car, the police president of Frankfurt and the *Regierungspräsident* of Cassel.

The British high commissioner, Sir Harold Stuart, was unable to agree to these proposals. Supported by the American, General Allen (who had no vote), he persuaded Monsieur Tirard to adopt a more conciliatory view of the incident. Sir Harold was convinced that Monsieur Tirard's original proposal had been due to pressure from Paris.[12]

The British high commissioner reported on 25 October that an interview[13] had taken place on 9 October between *Oberregierungsrat* Budding of the Cologne *Regierung* and

Colonel Ryan, chief representative of the high commission in Cologne. Dr Budding began by discussing separatism. He believed that this movement was beginning to make progress because of the unsettled state of Germany and the lack of confidence in the power of the German government to improve matters.

Encouragement was being received from the separatist movement in Bavaria. A number of Independent Socialists were being converted to this cause and some prominent industrialists in the area were beginning to consider the possibility of separation for the Rhineland.

His own view was that the formation of a Rhine state within the German federation would be advantageous, but he felt it should be opposed as it would undoubtedly come under French influence. He was firmly convinced that French policy was directed towards the annexation of the Rhineland. British policy, on the other hand, concentrating as it did on internal affairs, had allowed France to pursue its imperialist aims.

Dr Budding continued with the consideration that there was a preponderance of French opinion in the high commission. When Lord Kilmarnock, who had been appointed British high commissioner on 16 December 1920,[14] was presented with these views, he refuted the preponderance of French influence. The French high commissioner was under pressure from public opinion in France, from French commercial interests, from French military influence and, indeed, from his own government. The year 1920 closed, according to Lord Kilmarnock, in an atmosphere of unrest.

The first months of 1921 saw no developments of importance in the separatist movement. Dr Dorten and his followers seemed to have lost credibility in the political life of the Rhineland. Tirard had begun to downgrade Dorten, who had long received French funds. Tirard's patronage was cast towards Josef Smeets, editor and proprietor of the separatist journal the *Rheinische Republik.* At a meeting on 26 June 1921 in Bonn, 209 representatives of local groups in the Rhineland were present.[15] Speeches and resolutions passed were in support of a 'neutral' Rhineland and freedom from Prussia, with which state the Rhineland was joined in the German confederation. A programme for the circulation of propaganda for the 'Rheinishe Republik' was adopted. Smeets declared that the strength of the party was at least 145,000, thought by the British high commissioner to be a gross exaggeration.

As a counter measure to the Bonn meeting, representatives of Rhenish political parties had met in Königswinter on 9 June and passed a resolution against any plebiscite being held in the Rhineland.

In July 1921 Smeets became the focus of a lengthy, well-advertised legal wrangle. He was summoned to court on 4 July on a charge of slander; the case was postponed until December when Smeets was brought before the high commission. The legality of whether it was appropriate to bring such a case produced a tug of war between Monsieur Paul Tirard, hurriedly summoned from Paris and the newly appointed British high commissioner, Lord Kilmarnock.

Tirard had instructions from Monsieur Aristide Briand to secure Smeets's release; Kilmarnock was convinced that the French and Belgian arguments provided insufficient justification for this action. He asked that the matter be put to the vote. At this point, the Belgian high commissioner intervened to the effect that Smeets should be released only pending a decision in principle. Lord Kilmarnock was convinced that the British government was averse to interfering in the internal affairs of Germany and that it was anxious to preserve an attitude of strict neutrality with regard to domestic quarrels. He pointed out that even if it were in the interest of the Allies that a separate Rhineland Republic be established, the surest way of destroying the chances of such a movement would be if its leaders became suspect in the eyes of the Germans as regards Allied support.

Aware that the separatist movement enjoyed considerable sympathy in France, Monsieur Tirard was concerned to give satisfaction to French public opinion; he was also anxious to protect his own position as high commissioner. The American representative on the commission supported his British colleague throughout the discussion. Smeets was released on 9 December and appeared before a German court, but the episode was not over and he appeared in the following year. On 15 December, the British government told Lord Kilmarnock that his action had been approved.

The Smeets case dragged on well into 1922. On 11 January Monsieur Tirard called his colleagues together for an unofficial meeting and, after a good deal of discussion, it was agreed that the German authorities should be informed that the cases pending against Smeets would be tried in the courts, but that the high commission maintained the right to intervene before any sentence were executed. Monsieur Tirard remarked that he regarded any term of imprisonment as unjustified. Smeets was tried on 15 February, 3 March, and 12 and 19 June and he was found guilty of all charges. In August 1922, the French high commissioner stated that he was bound by his instructions to propose that the German sentences pronounced against Smeets should not be allowed to be put into execution. The British high commissioner said that his instructions were in a directly contrary direction. The Belgian high commissioner said he could not, in view of the excited state of public opinion in Belgium over recent murders at Oberkassel, do anything but vote with the French.

The high commission met again on 28 September. After a long discussion, a vote was taken. The French and Belgian high commissioners voted in favour of a resolution deciding that 'no steps be taken to proceed with the execution of the sentences passed against Herr Smeets' on four appearances in court. Colonel Ryan (acting British high commissioner) voted against it, supported by the vote-less American general. Public protests by the German judiciary followed, together with a good deal of anti-Allied propaganda.

During these months of debate about his future, Smeets had been energetic in the pursuance of the cause of Rhineland separatism, with the result that the press of the territory approached the matter with some nervousness. He established branches of his party at Wiesbaden, Kaiserlauten, Koblenz, Sölingen and Düsseldorf and encouraged those already established at Bonn, Trier, Aix-la-Chapelle and Mainz; at the same time, the central government and political parties were equally active in carrying on counter-propaganda. In May, the German government sent a letter to higher German officials in the British zone warning them that the proclamation of a republic might be expected. The press reported Allied complicity in separatist intrigues, and considered that Britain might approve a plebiscite on the establishment of a Rhineland Republic. German trade union leaders expressed their fears that the British government, in its desire to reach a compromise with France, might be disposed to make a concession with French Rhineland policy.

Herr Hartig, one of their number, said that the chief fear of the moment was lest the separatists should proclaim a republic and the French military authorities, under the pretext of preserving law and order, should prevent the provisional Rhenish government from being turned out. A separatist government, once established, could be extended by French military influence throughout the whole occupied territory. Among others, the cry went up that France's real aim in the Rhineland was annexation. Unrest remained, and nervousness over a possible outcome was the atmosphere at the end of 1922.

The murder of the German foreign minister, Walter Rathenau, by right-wing extremists in June 1922, indicated the extent of the troubles in Germany as a whole. (Matthais Erzberger, the German deputy who had signed the armistice, had already been murdered in August 1921.) It has been calculated[16] that between 1918 and 1922, organizations of the right were responsible for 354 politically motivated murders.

Nothing much was heard of Dorten in the early days of 1923, but Smeets was active in the Eifel (the area between Koblenz and Trier). He began to invite applications for posts in the new Rhineland administration, which he declared would soon be established. An attempted assassination of Smeets took place in Cologne on 17 March 1923. A man armed with a pistol entered his house and shot at him; he killed his secretary, then shot again and wounded Smeets in the head. The assailant made good his escape. The press did not make much of the incident, but reports were received of the statements of certain French politicians pressing for the 'internationalization' of the Rhineland as a means of creating security for France. The French high commissioner, under pressure from Paris, wished the chief of police to be suspended and the case against Smeets's opponents to be transferred from a German to a military court. The British high commissioner was able to thrust the issue into the background.

The separatists held a mass meeting at Düsseldorf on 30 September 1923; the supply of special trains enabled thousands of members, mainly from the least educated sectors of the population, to attend. Fighting between communists, separatists and the German police interrupted the demonstration; 17 were killed and 400 wounded. Rumours of a proclamation of a Rhineland Republic had preceded the meeting. Lord Kilmarnock, the British high commissioner, had been apprised of this possibility, and he asked his government for instructions about what to do if this should come to pass. He was told carefully to avoid committing His Majesty's Government to recognition of any new situation. The troops of occupation would be employed in maintaining order, as far as possible, and in preventing any act of violence that might threaten. The German press termed the incident the *blutbad*. The French authorities were blamed for having allowed the meeting of so many (between 15,000 and 20,000) to take place.

A Rhineland Republic was proclaimed at Aix-la-Chapelle on 21 October 1923 by a branch of the separatist party called *Frei Rheinland*. It was led by Leo Deckers and had ties with Colonel Paul Reul and Pierre Nothomb of the Belgian nationalist organization, *Comité de Politique Nationale*; it had been launched with the aid of a Belgian called Lieutenant Peters. The aim was declared 'as the creation of a Belgian sphere of influence in the lower Rhine to prevent "French encirclement"'. The German police appeared to have been under the command of the Belgians, for they offered no resistance and cooperated with the separatists in keeping order. The separatist flag was hoisted over government buildings after they had been taken over.

During the week that followed, a separatist *putsch*, which was led by Adam Dorten, Josef Matthes and Herr von Metzen, along with several thousand armed followers, took place in towns in the French zone. There were some casualties at Bonn; at Mainz the French military were able to restore order and disarm the separatists who were more successful at Trier. The post office and government buildings were occupied and the police disarmed. At Koblenz, after having hoisted their flag on the old palace on 23 October, the separatists were forced to haul it down. My mother later told me of her experience of having been caught by the demonstrations while shopping, and she had slipped down a side street, and swiftly headed for home. A second attempt was made on 25 October, by separatists supported by French troops. Several hundred of them arrived by train and took possession of their objectives, the *Rathaus*, palace, and post and telegraph offices. Separatists and French soldiers delivered placards throughout the town that proclaimed the Rhineland Republic and gave its reasons as follows:[17] 'To save the Rhine at the eleventh hour from complete misery through the fault of Prussia, and to save it from a Radical revolution from the Left, the Independent Rhinelanders have taken over the civil administration. ... The Rhineland Republic is proclaimed. The Provisional Government is constituted.'

A similar pattern was followed at Bonn, where equally coarse hooligan elements had been admitted into the town. While separatists were due to remain in the French zone for the time being, in the zone the Belgians administered the movement began to collapse. The Belgian high commissioner ordered the separatists to evacuate public buildings and hand their arms to the Belgian military and this action, which he took entirely on his own initiative, was successful. Whereas the Belgian occupying forces had earlier shown interest in the separatist movement, this demonstrated a change of tactics. The Belgian high commissioner requested of the British that inter-Allied deliberations on the matter of the Rhineland Republic movement should take place. Raymond Poincaré, with the knowledge of British views, did not care for this suggestion. The nationalist party in Belgium was in favour of a separated Rhineland, and kept in close touch with German separatists.

The British government's policy in relation to separatism

in the Rhineland had been made clear by the end of October 1923. It informed[18] the British high commissioner and ambassadors in Paris, Brussels and Rome that setting up independent states carved out of territories within the existing frontiers of Germany might have very grave consequences. The British high commissioner was told that there seemed to be no reason why the Rhineland high commission should not come to decisions about this matter, so long as the safety of the armies of occupation was not jeopardized. It was not in accordance with the Rhineland Agreement that the 'Provisional Separatist Administration', which had installed itself at Koblenz, should issue decrees and enjoy armed support. Lord Kilmarnock was instructed to press for the rearming of the German police and the disarming of all unauthorized persons by that body.

In a note to Monsieur Tirard of 26 October 1923, the deputy British high commissioner called attention to the way in which Koblenz had fallen under the authority of the separatists. Armed bands of men had been allowed to move through the streets without any interference from the French troops, who were in control of the German police. On 24 October the *Bürgermeister* of Koblenz and others had been temporarily deported and a full inquiry had been requested. However, as he left for Paris to consult his government, this was something that Monsieur Tirard refused to provide. Feelings had run high in the high commission; the Belgian high commissioner later explained confidentially to his British colleague that Belgium was not in a strong enough position to oppose its French neighbour on a continual basis.

While every few days, one or two small villages were still falling under the control of separatists, there were signs of disagreement and disunion among their leaders. This was due partly to an anti-separatist incident at Honnef in which the local population attacked a group of separatists; a pitched battle took place in which fourteen separatists were killed and four were badly wounded. French military forces arrived when the fighting was over. The news of the affray was widely reported in the press. Separatist leaders, in their various factions, who had installed the 'Provisional Separatist Government' in Koblenz and appointed themselves to posts within it, began to disagree. Matthes sent a letter to Monsieur Tirard on 27 November, which told him that the 'Provisional Government' had been dissolved. It was no surprise, for it was clear that the separatists could no longer keep the positions they had held.

Monsieur Tirard began to modify his attitude towards the political figures in the occupied territory. Whereas he had informed leaders of the Socialist and Centre parties in Cologne that France would accept nothing less than an independent Rhineland state, on 3 November 1923 he said that he was ready to negotiate, on the basis of federalism, for the formation of a federal Rhenish state within the German Reich. This attitude no doubt owed much to the fact that the separatist movement, as far as the Rhineland Province was concerned, was moribund. The French could not continue to support a body that held no semblance of organization and whose members had become mere isolated bands.

The Palatinate

Although the separatist movement on the lower Rhine had proved a failure, the movement in the Palatinate (the French zone spreading from the Upper Mosel to Bavaria) had taken its place. The ideals of Dorten were being upheld by three leading Palatinate socialists: Hoffmann, a member of the *Reichstag*, Wagner, a Hamburg lawyer and Kleefost, a mayor of Ludwigshafen. They made contact with General de Metz, the French delegate-general in that zone, and negotiated successfully on 3 November 1923 for the establishment of an autonomous palatinate with a provisional government. A few day later, armed bands of separatists began active operations in the area.

Separatists took possession of public buildings at Kaiserlauten on 5 November; French troops used the tactics that 'had been employed with success' on earlier occasions, with the result that the movement spread quickly through the province. The British government instructed its ambassador in Paris to protest against the action of the French local authorities. On 14 November the German government then protested against the support being given to a rabble 'armed with cudgels, revolvers, and in some cases, with rifles'. In a second protest on 23 November, the German government complained that General de Metz had declared that the government of the free Palatinate, which had been established by Franz Josef Heinz-Orbis, the leader of the separatists, was a *fait accompli* and must be recognized by the French government.

The same Heinz-Orbis, head of the so-called 'Palatinate Provisional Government', was assassinated in a café in Speyer in the French zone on 9 January 1924. At the same sitting as the high commission was given details of Heinz-Orbis's murder, Paul Tirard mentioned that there was a strong suspicion that members of a secret nationalist society named *Treuband* had committed the crime. This secret society owed its origin to the notorious Ritter von Eberlein, chief of the *Fürsorgstelle* of Heidelberg. He went on to discuss various other nationalist societies in the Rhineland – the *Jung Deutschen Orden*, the *Deutschnational Jugendbund* and *Stahlhelm*, a militant but conventionally nationalistic ex-service organization – and emphasized their potential danger. In future secret societies were to become an increasing menace.

After some wrangling, the high commission resolved to stop respecting the autonomous government's laws. The Belgian high commissioner played into British government hands by staying in Brussels on the day, 24 January 1924, when the high commission was to have come to a final decision on the Palatinate decrees, thereby affecting the voting.

In the meantime, Robert Clive, who was the consul-general at Munich, had been deputed to pay an extensive visit to the Palatinate. He arrived in Heidelberg on 14 January and travelled on to Mannheim where he met the Catholic bishop, the head of the Protestant Church, the secretaries of all the significant trade unions, journalists, agriculturalists, mayors, lawyers, industrialists and the various representatives of the working communities. They appeared to give abundant evidence that the French authorities were supporting the autonomous government. Clive proceeded to Landau and to a further tour of the Palatinate. The British government received his report on

23 January. In every place he visited he 'was told that if the occupying authorities withdrew their support ... for twenty-four hours, there would not be one separatist left' in the province.

The situation in the Palatinate became very disturbed. Anti-separatists began to take reprisals for what they had suffered and a near state of anarchy developed, particularly at Pirmasens, a town of 42,000 inhabitants. An attack by about 600 men, variously armed, took place on 12 February 1924 on the building in which separatists were lodged; they defended themselves by shooting into the crowd, but were forced to surrender because the building had been set on fire; a number of them were burnt and 12 were massacred. Only four French soldiers were stationed in the town, but reinforcements arrived later in the night. The high commission declared a state of siege on 13 February. A similar conflict occurred at Kaiserlauten – with separatists and anti-separatists fighting it out. According to the reckoning of the representative of the Reich at Munich, the strength of the separatists had been between 10,000 and 12,000 men, with about 1200 firearms.

It took almost a year before normal conditions returned to the Palatinate. The Rhineland Republic movement foundered for the same reason as in the Rhineland Province – a lack of local commitment. The dislike on the part of the predominantly Catholic Rhineland at being shackled in a federal system with Protestant Prussia, was not strong enough to create a cohesive force for change. It was noticed during the course of separatist coups, that few of the attackers were local men; the practice of 'rent a mob' had been employed. Moreover, the few leaders were on the whole of poor quality, and seemingly unwelcome as liberators. British and American support was nil and that of France, which can be interpreted as one more attempt to buy security, intermittent.

Chapter 4
AMERICAN FORCES LEAVE THE RHINE (1922–23)

Keith Nelson's incisive book *Victors Divided* presents a thoughtful account, not only of the American part of the occupation of the Rhineland, but of its important political background. To go back to the beginning, he maintains that the Americans in 1917 and 1918 'completely disregarded or overlooked the possibility of postwar military occupation in Germany'. The explanation Nelson gives is 'that Americans were simply not ready to think of themselves as part of the European world'.[1] He continues to maintain that 'neither isolationist or internationalists … saw a need to give much thought to the future of Germany. To them the victory in battle was all that was necessary.' By the time of the armistice, however, which neither 'completely disarmed' nor 'compelled Germany's ultimate capitulation', it seemed obvious that some military sanctions were required. When President Wilson read the terms of the armistice to an assembled Congress on 11 November, his reference to an occupation received sustained applause.

At the same time, he became uneasy on account of the enthusiasm shown for the idea by the French. Especially of anxiety were Clemenceau's aspirations about the separation of the Rhineland from the rest of Germany. The United States had eventually to agree to the occupation of the Rhineland, giving in to French pressure, and to restrain France, as much as any other cause. The Germans were informed on 5 November 1918 that peace could be promised on the basis of President Wilson's 14 points, already described, and armistice terms set out by Marshal Foch. By 8 November, when representatives of the Allies and Germans met near Compiégne, those present recalled that it was the occupation of the Rhineland that was the most painful of the armistice conditions accorded to the former enemy.[2]

In accepting the Rhineland occupation the USA, unlike its allies, had no previously conceived aims about how to control its territory. After some early administrative errors due to inexperience, the Americans set out to be benign occupiers, allowing the Germans to govern themselves under the arrangements set out in Article Five of the Rhineland Agreement. But, from the start, the smooth outlook was disturbed by actions of the French. The communications of Marshal Foch to his commanders regarding military government included a large number of models of specific regulations. One of Douglas Haig's staff officers was reported as saying that 'The only possible way for a German to avoid contravening one or other of Foch's many by-laws, will be to stay in bed.'

Old differences of opinion between General Pershing and Marshal Foch were ignited several times during the early occupation period. The size of the American contingent was a source of quarrels, as was the occupation of Luxemburg. The Americans triumphed in that one, but certainly not in all. The term of office for whosoever commanded the American forces was dogged by what Nelson called 'a struggle to ward off French interference'. In his *The Rhineland Occupation,*[3] General Allen wrote of the attempt to break free of French oversight in April 1920:

> In the latter part of March, the House of Representatives moved by the stirring events on the Rhine, requested by resolution:
>
> > the extent of the authority exercised over American military forces now stationed in German territory by Marshal Foch how far their activity may be directed without express orders from the President of the United States. The President answered that Marshal Foch 'has no authority over United States troops in Germany, nor can anyone direct their activities without express orders from the President of the United States'.

On the political front, President Wilson had successfully sold his concept of a League of Nations to the European powers, who incorporated it into the Treaty of Versailles.

Before he suffered his stroke in October 1919, he had failed to convince the American Senate of the value of a treaty that had provisions for a league, for fear of involvement in the affairs of Europe. He evoked the farewell speech of George Washington, given on 17 September 1796, held in high regard by Americans.

> Europe has a set of primary interests, which to us have none, or a very remote relation. Hence she must be engaged in frequent controversies, the causes of which are essentially foreign to our concerns. Hence, therefore, it must be unwise in us to implicate ourselves by artificial ties, in the ordinary vicissitudes of her politics, or the ordinary combinations and collisions of her friendships or enmities.

Ratification of the treaty was therefore blocked. He also failed to recover his health.

Henry 'Cabot' Lodge (1856–1924) entered the Senate in 1893 as a representative of the Republican Party's conservative wing, and remained there for the rest of his life. He was sharply critical of Woodrow Wilson's prosecution of the war. In the congressional elections of 1918, the Republicans gained control of both the House and the Senate. Cabot Lodge became the chairman of the Senate Committee on Foreign Relations and Senate majority leader. He led the fight against ratification of the Treaty of Versailles, largely because it included a league of nations.

In 1920 Lodge played a leading role in securing the Republican nomination for Warren Harding and in Harding's victory, thereby quashing the Wilson attitude towards America's role in the postwar world. Harding, who was born in Ohio in 1865, had been the publisher of a newspaper and was well known for his undeviating Republicanism and vibrant speaking voice. In 1920 he won the presidential election by an unprecedented landslide of 60 per cent of the popular vote. His inaugural address of 4 March 1921 included words that made his attitude towards American involvement in the affairs of Europe abundantly clear.

> In the beginning, the Old World scoffed at our experiment; today our foundations of political and social belief stand unshaken, a precious inheritance to ourselves, an inspiring example of freedom and civilization to all mankind. Let us express renewed and strengthened devotion, in grateful reverence for the immortal beginning, and utter confidence in the supreme fulfilment.
>
> The recorded progress of our Republic, materially and spiritually, in itself proves the wisdom of the inherited policy of non-involvement in Old World affairs. Confident of our ability to work out our own destiny, and jealously guarding our right to do so, we seek no part in directing the destinies of the Old World. We do not mean to be entangled. We will accept no responsibility except as our own conscience and judgment, in each instance, may determine.

America's continued presence in Germany would seem to be doomed.

A new era had begun for the United States Army on the Rhine with the arrival of its new commander, General Henry Allen, who took the place of the other wartime generals in July 1919. Although some of his attributes have already been mentioned, his career described by Heath Twichell Jr[4] is worthy of recall, for it is as much through his own experiences that the US Army of the Rhine emerged as it did.

Henry Tureman Allen was born in Kentucky of land-owning stock; he was the thirteenth child in a family of fourteen. His strong physical characteristics (he was tall and good-looking and could jump into a saddle from a flat-foot start) certainly came into their own during his years in the Rhineland. After graduating from the Military Academy at West Point, he proceeded to Alaska on a dangerous two-year expedition to the Yukon River territory, mapping as he went, well above the Arctic Circle.

A period in Russia to learn the language followed and in due course he was appointed to the Military Academy at West Point to teach French. He became military attaché at the American legation in St Petersburg in 1889 where he was the only member of the staff who could speak French, German and Russian. Allen's appointment as military attaché in the United States embassy in Berlin was a natural consequence. In November 1899, he brushed up his Spanish and left for the Philippines. A brutal guerrilla war was put down and Allen became military governor of one of the larger islands and organizer of the Philippine constabulary, a force that eventually grew to 10,000 men.

Back in the USA he was given command of the 13th cavalry with the rank of full colonel and was sent to the war that had broken out in Mexico in 1914. In August 1917 he was promoted to the rank of brigadier-general and was put in command of the 90th division in Texas, a National Guard division. He was ordered to bring the division up to strength and to sail for France in mid-June 1918.

On 15 August, Allen issued Field Order No. 1. The American First Army was about to make its debut under General Pershing. At 5.00 a.m. on 12 September, the men of Allen's two brigades went 'over the top' and nine hours later all his units had achieved their objectives, although they had taken heavy casualties: these were men whom Allen would not bring back to Texas. He was accredited with having made a reconnaissance on horseback across the front when enemy fire continued and his companion was killed. Allen stayed on in Europe 'to take what was probably the most interesting, potentially one of the most important, and certainly the most glamorous assignments in the postwar army'.[5]

But in spite of his natural talents and skills, already described, to raise the physical and educational standards in his army, Allen's position was not secure. In one of President Harding's speeches in 1920, someone in the crowd asked him what he intended to do with 'the boys in Germany'. He replied that as soon as a formal peace was declared 'we can be sure they will be coming home'. A Treaty between the United States and Germany was signed on 29 August 1921; there was no move so far to recall the American army on the Rhine. General Allen continued his energetic programme: consorting with other Allied commanders, ceremonial events, the improvement of trade and conditions of life for the population in the American zone and his own hard physical exercise: hunting and polo.

The State Department had appointed Allen to succeed Pierrepont Noyes to represent America at high commission meetings, but not as commissioner. He achieved some success as a diplomat and could be relied on to lend support to British and Belgian commissioners. Keith Nelson writes that none of Allen's policies was 'the result of formal instructions from his own government. His decisions were his own; more and more evidence piled up as to the value of the American forces to their British counterparts'. In July 1921, Malcolm Robertson wrote to Marquess Curzon of Kedleston (British foreign secretary 1919): 'As regards the American troops, I feel that the consequences of their withdrawal might easily be of so grave a nature that I beg your Lordship to consider whether it might not be possible to make earnest and unofficial representations in Washington with a view to their retention.'[6]

The strength of the AFG remained at approximately 15,000 for 1920. In the four months between Harding's election and inauguration, Woodrow Wilson was able to order the reduction to 6500. It was further reduced to 1000 and more and more French troops moved into what was nominally the American zone, though under Allen's command.

On 22 March 1922, General Allen recorded in his diary that: 'A definitive cable came today from Washington saying that the President had decided to bring back to the States all American forces by 1 July, asking me to submit a schedule of transports.'[7]

By a curious coincidence, this date marked my birth in the American Military Hospital in Koblenz. A photograph in my mother's album (it was her birthday; we shared the date) shows a nurse holding me, aged nine days, and Virginia McGregor, aged four days, daughter of an American officer's wife. My American birth certificate is headed American Forces in Germany – Headquarters Station Hospital Koblenz, and signed by an obstetrician, Emery R. Neff, Major Medical Corps US Army and by Francis M. Fitts, Major Medical Corps US Army, Adjutant. My father took the precaution of registering my birth at the British consulate general at Cologne also, so that my status as a British subject could be established. This became of importance during the Second World War.

My certificate of baptism is American also, as having taken place in the chapel of the palace in Koblenz (lent temporarily to the American forces), on Sunday 30 April 1922, signed by Edmund P. Easterbrook, senior chaplain, American Forces in Germany. His name appeared frequently in Allen's journal.

On hearing the news of the impending American departure, the Allies took action: Monsieur Tirard, the French high commissioner, went at once to Paris to try to persuade his government to act. Two days later, Allen received a telegram from the American embassy in London, cautioning him to say nothing of the move. He comments that the Washington administration was apparently finding it difficult to make a decision between the claims of the situation on the Rhine and the demands of political exigency at home.[8]

On 3 June 1922 Allen received a telegram from the US

War Department authorizing him to remain in Germany until further notice with a force not to exceed 1200, including officers. Members of the American army were, according to Allen, elated. Dr Gustav Stresemann, German foreign minister, who was to play a major part in relations between Germany and the other European powers, called on the general by appointment on 9 October and expressed his views on current international problems; he felt that the sum demanded of Germany for reparations should be reduced, which was the next great issue. During the next two months Allen received disquieting news about French intentions in the Ruhr and tried to intervene in a diplomatic manner.

An overwhelming sequence of events took place during the second week of January 1923. According to Allen's diary, he received a letter from General Degoutte on 7 January, telling him of a preliminary movement of troops prior to their entering the Ruhr; Allen at once informed the US State Department by telegram. Two days earlier, on 5 January, President Harding stated at a press conference that the American administration was in favour of withdrawing its troops from the Rhine, but that Belgium, Britain and France were in favour of their retention.

During the course of the evening of 10 January when Allen was hosting a dinner party, his aides called him away several times to answer the telephone: the recall of his troops from Germany had been expedited. Next day, 11 January, he received the confirmatory telegram and recorded that it had been four years and two months, to the day, since the signing of the armistice. A ship, the *St Mihiel,* would sail immediately to Bremen or Hamburg (in the event it was Antwerp) to transport all US troops back to their native land.

The connection between this departure and the French entry into the Ruhr has been much debated on all sides and, because of the unconvincing timing, it is difficult to determine what exactly this might have been. Clearly, the secretary of state Charles Evans Hughes was intending to use the possible withdrawal of the American army as a lever to prevent French action into the Ruhr. But he was overtaken by an act of the Senate.

On 8 January Hughes told the French ambassador that if Poincaré moved French troops into the Ruhr, the departure from Germany of the American army would follow. But he was, however, too late. On 7 January Senator Reed introduced a new resolution in the Senate demanding that US troops in Germany should head for home. The Senate passed Reed's measure by a vote of 57 to 6. League of Nations Democrats had joined with isolationist Republicans because 'both agreed that only trouble could result if the AFG remained in Europe'.[9] On that side of the Atlantic minds were made up; Allen's army would leave the Rhine.

It only remained for Allen to say, and receive, his farewells. The population of Koblenz was said to have expressed its regrets at the departure of the American troops who had done so much for them. Allen wrote that 'To me the outstanding feature of this farewell is the genuine sorrow depicted in the faces of both allies and Germans.'[10]

Chancellor Wilhelm Cuno sent a particularly flattering set of sentiments. As he put it: 'The German government appreciated highly the spirit in which you have administered the authority vested in you.'

Monsieur Tirard, not to be outdone, and putting aside earlier brushes, wrote a characteristic piece in the French army newspaper *Echo du Rhin*, which referred to the 'eminent soldier and accomplished gentleman, General Allen'.

Finally, on 24 January 1923, at noon, the American flag was lowered for the last time on the tower of the castle of Ehrenbreitstein, overlooking the Rhine. Straight away the French flag was hoisted, in its stead, to mark the beginning of the French occupation of the former American zone. This is as I remember Koblenz, full of French soldiers in their (at that time) pale blue uniforms. The British high commissioner, Lord Kilmarnock, and the Belgian, Baron Rolin Jacquemyns, absented themselves from the ceremony to register their regret.[11] The departing troops, with brass band, marched between rows of French soldiers lining the route as they made their way to Koblenz railway station for an onward journey by train, and embarkation for the USA from Antwerp.

The same evening at a dinner given by Monsieur Tirard in Allen's honour, the French high commissioner made his valedictory speech. He could not resist his customary mention of the French flag, which had now replaced the American one, and he continued: '*C'est avec une profonde émotion, mon general, que je salue une dernière fois vos troupes qui ont vécu avec les nôtres et que je salue leur glorieux chef. Je lève mon verre en l'honneur de l'armée americaine et du général Allen.*'[12]

Chapter 5 FRENCH AND BELGIAN TROOPS ENTER THE RUHR

It has been suggested that it was Lloyd George who, during the preparations of the Versailles peace treaty, recognized that no precise figure for reparations to be paid by Germany should be calculated in the disturbed atmosphere of 1919. 'He therefore urged that the treaty should merely state the principle of Germany's liability and that the sum should be fixed later after a cool examination of her financial resources.'[1]

In the following years a 'precise figure' for reparations and a 'cool examination' were to become equally elusive. It was not until 1921 that the Reparations Commission set up by the Treaty of Versailles arrived at a sum for Germany to be required to pay: 132,000 million gold marks (£6600 million). By the year 1922 it had paid nothing.

Britain was prepared to accept a two-year stay on cash payment from Germany, but France would not agree. Poincaré, who had been the prime minister of France since January 1922, was convinced that Germany had the capacity to pay, in spite of the financial disaster then current; (on 1 August 1922 there were 2850 German marks to a pound sterling; by 5 September 1922 this figure had risen to 6525, and by the end of the year it was 40,000). Quite apart from Germany's default in terms of money, there was a shortfall in the delivery of the reparations' quota of coal and wood; the latter was needed for the production of telegraph poles. A commentator murmured that 'Not since the Trojan horse has wood been so misused.'[2]

Poincaré, intending to seize Ruhr coal as a 'productive pledge', occupied the area. A likely subsidiary motive would have been to reduce the power of Germany so as to increase the security of France. On 11 January 1923, therefore, French and Belgian troops with a party of Italian civil engineers (no soldiers) entered the Ruhr. It was a region so-called on account of the River Ruhr, which flowed for 60 miles, mainly through Westphalia, into the Rhine; it was an area of considerable natural resources, mineral wealth and industrialization. It provided 85 per cent of German coal and other raw materials.

The first moves occupied a line: this went from Kupferdreh to Steele, Kray, Katerberg, Horst, Bottrop, Sterkrade and Dinslaken. The Franco–Belgian–Italian mission of control (so-called as a primitive disguise of its purely military character) was established at Essen on the morning of 11 January. Presumably warned of its impending arrival, the coal syndicate at Essen had fled to Hamburg; only that portion of the syndicate that dealt with the reparations coal remained at Essen. The German government then issued an order forbidding the delivery of any reparations coal and the remainder of the Essen syndicate left the city. French and Belgian troops moved forward again to occupy a line embracing Bochum, Gelsenkirchen and Recklinghausen. The German government issued further instructions on 16 January that no deliveries of coal were to be conveyed to France or Belgium, even on payment. In response, French and Belgian forces moved to Dortmund.

The intention to avoid a military confrontation in the Ruhr failed. By 22 January 1923 French troops in the area numbered 45,000 and Belgians 5000; by May the figure had risen to approximately 51,000 and 9000 respectively. A control commission of engineers, known at first as the *Mission Coste,* afterwards as the *Mission interalliée de Contrôle des Usines et des Mines* (MICUM) was sent to the Ruhr to supervise the reparations coal deliveries and other 'productive pledges'. 'The German local authorities relegated the desired economic nature of the action to the background. The French and Belgian governments found themselves obliged to give their action a military and coercive character.'[3]

The French immediately declared martial law in the newly occupied territory; German officials were put under military authority and the French gendarmerie replaced the police. An unexpected development occurred when the German government under Chancellor Wilhelm Cuno ordered the people of the Ruhr to establish a regime of passive resistance, applicable to every man, woman and child who should refuse 'to lift a pin for the invader'.[4]

Germany gained sympathy from world opinion, but at considerable cost to its own economy. As for the population, the British high commission report for 1923 relates that: 'Conditions in the Ruhr resembled to a large extent those which existed during the last war in any of the districts lying immediately behind the danger area. The German administrative authorities had been removed and expulsions *en masse* of railwaymen and others were a daily occurrence. No newspapers appeared; no telegraph or telephone service functioned.'[5]

Feelings between French nationals and Germans in the Ruhr became exceedingly bitter. French officers and officials living in hotels were left without any domestic help and it became the norm for staff to refuse to serve them in restaurants and in many of the shops. Wholesale expulsions from the area into unoccupied Germany meant that, with their homes confiscated and inhabited by Frenchmen, those concerned became destitute.

On 17 May a serious affray between miners on strike, led by communist *Hunderschaften* and police, occurred in Dortmund. By the end of the month more than 250,000 men had been affected. All together 40 men were killed and 300 injured in the disturbances. The French were blamed, having expelled the police force. The French organization MICUM took possession of the 'Viktor' collieries near Dortmund in the summer of 1923. Further occupation included that of Wesel and Emmerich by Belgian troops; in June, occupation by Frenchmen was extended to include the Rhine harbour of Karlsruhe.

It was the railways of the occupied Rhineland and Ruhr that suffered the greatest upheaval as the result of the French action. Late on 6 January 1923 General Degoutte, French commander-in-chief of the Allied force in the Rhineland, had warned General Godley, commander of the British army in Cologne, that French troops were to be concentrated by rail in the area east of Düsseldorf, beginning on 8 January and suggested: 'that the railway over which these troops would travel through the British zone should be guarded. … Accordingly 6½ companies of British infantry were sent to guard the six lines in question. They remained in position until 14 January and in the seven days, 176 trains of French troops passed through to the Ruhr.'[6]

At 2.00 a.m. on 24 January General Godley was told that General Degoutte feared that there would be a railway strike in the British, as well as in the French and Belgian zones. A request was made for 750 French railway employees to be distributed along the railways of the British zone, but it was refused. General Godley's threat to withdraw the British army from the Rhineland put an end to any thoughts of a strike in the British area. In the Ruhr the standstill prevailed, with railwaymen acting under the instructions of the Cuno government.

The French reacted by importing engine drivers and signalmen from France. The French-directed railway, called the *Régie,* operated under very difficult conditions because frequent attempts were being made to sabotage the lines and level crossings. Its operations included the railways in the occupied territory west of the Rhine, with the exception of the British enclave where Germans remained at work as before.[7] A pact, known as the Godley–Payot pact (after the two generals who had secured it) permitted ten French transport trains and two supply trains to pass through the British zone, in both directions, each day.

The seizure of the 'productive pledges' and the lack of cooperation of the British in the Ruhr episode, raised the question of what attitude the British high commissioner should adopt. Lord Kilmarnock considered that a withdrawal of the British occupying force would be unwise. So long as the British army remained on the Rhine it could act as a check on the French to some extent and it could also exercise a direct influence on the course of events; if it left, the French would be free to carry out their policy of establishing an autonomous Rhineland Republic.[8] Lord Kilmarnock expressed his conviction that it was possible for him to maintain cordial relations with his French and Belgian colleagues, in spite of the difficult situation in which he was placed.

Although Britain's recent action had been met with disapproval, the British government decided that a policy of 'benevolent neutrality' should be adopted with respect to the maintenance of relations with France. In the Rhineland high commission, Lord Kilmarnock was precluded from taking any decisions that might arise on the matter of the Ruhr.

On the diplomatic front, two personalities emerge at this point who were both to play a prominent part in relations between Britain and Germany. One of these was the British ambassador at Berlin, Lord D'Abernon. Born in 1857, the son of an Anglican vicar, he joined the foreign service as an interpreter and failed to take up an offered appointment. He became a governor of the Imperial Ottoman Bank, then the member of parliament for Exeter in 1889. His career took a curious turn when he became chairman of the Thoroughbred Horse Breeders' Association between 1917 and 1932; and later, in 1928, he joined the Racecourse Betting Control Board. He was appointed to Berlin in 1920 and was also a member of the Privy Council. Although he was not a professional diplomat, 'his knowledge of currency and economics was greater than [that of] anyone in the Foreign Service'.[9] He pursued good relations with the leaders of Germany.

The most distinguished statesman of his generation on the German side was Gustav Stresemann, the German foreign minister in the Cuno government and a member of the German People's Party (*Deutsche Volkspartei* or DVP). He entered the *Reichstag* in 1907 when he was in his twenties and was the youngest member. 'With energy and ability to organize, an able speaker in the *Reichstag*, and expert in social policy and on economic aspects of foreign policy, he was in demand in various parts of the country.'[10]

By the summer of 1923 the Weimar Republic was in grave trouble. Various groups, including Hitler's NSDAP, were threatening to take advantage, even to the extent of causing a civil war, of the German government's precarious situation. On 20 August Chancellor Wilhelm Cuno resigned.

President Frederich Ebert then asked Gustav Stresemann, who was then aged 45, to become the German chancellor. He recognized that passive resistance had to be abandoned and Lord D'Abernon, the British ambassador, freely gave him his support. On 24 September 1923, at a conference held between the German government and representatives of the Rhineland and the Ruhr, it was unanimously agreed that, given the present state of German finances, it had become impossible to pursue a policy of passive resistance; the cost of this decision was the fall of the Stresemann government. Wilhelm Marx became chancellor, with Stresemann in his distinctive role of foreign minister. His supreme ambition was to see a strong Germany, rid of foreign troops; and he was almost to achieve his goal.

On 30 November 1923 the Reparations Commission created two committees of experts with a view to alleviating some of the problems associated with payment. The first was designed to make suggestions about the resources and capacity of Germany to pay reparations and to stabilize the currency. The name of the appointed chairman, Brigadier-General Charles Dawes, would become well-known in the next stage of the reparations issue and the so-called Dawes Plan. The second committee, with Reginald McKenna as its chairman, was responsible for estimating the amount of exported German capital and bringing it back to Germany.

French and Belgian troops remained in the Ruhr for a further 15 months, at which point diplomatic negotiations (see Chapter 5) enabled them to leave. It had been a time of disaster for Germany and no great help to France. Britain also was affected economically because it was dependent for trade upon a strong Germany. When, on 15 November 1923, Stresemann introduced a new form of currency, the

Rentenmark, some improvement followed. The issue by a *Rentenbank* of 500 gold mark interest bearing *Rentenbriefe* was secured on agricultural industries and the banks of Germany.

But there were sinister elements abroad also. Hitler was dictating[11] *Mein Kampf* in prison, following his failed *putsch* in 1923. The first Nazi *Reichsparteitag* (party rally) had been held in Munich from 27 to 29 January 1923, with an attendance of approximately six thousand men.[12]

> From now on, National Socialist battalions were assembled again and again in such localities. … The *SA* [*Sturmabteilungen*] had grown more and more into its task and so had moved further away from the character of a senseless and unimportant defence movement and risen to the level of a living organization of strength of a new German state. …
>
> The occupation of the Ruhr by the French in the first months of 1923, had in the following period a great significance for the development of the SA.

He wrote of the influence the occupation of the Ruhr had on future developments in Germany. 'Now at length there would be an end to the cowardly policy of retreat, and that with this a definite task would fall to the combat leagues.'

Hitler proceeded to describe how, in the spring and summer of 1923, the *Sturmabteilungen* was reshaped 'into a military fighting organization'.[13]

Chapter 6
DISARMAMENT, REPARATIONS AND LOCARNO (1924–26)

On the matter of reparations, the move of the French army into the Ruhr cured nothing. Increased bitterness between France and Germany and economic failure on both sides were the result. Moreover, other requirements of the Treaty of Versailles remained unresolved, particularly German disarmament.

Disarmament

The military, naval and air clauses of the treaty were drawn up with a view to limiting armaments in all nations, particularly to compel Germany, which had achieved a considerable growth in armaments, to begin limitation. The overall aim was to prevent the danger of future aggression by Germany, though still allowing it a military force sufficient to maintain internal order. The execution of those articles of the treaty that dealt with German disarmament was placed under the supervision of the International Military Commission of Control (IMCC), responsible to the Conference of Ambassadors, which had been appointed the treaty's official executor.[1] Naval and air forces were forbidden.

Owing to the disturbed state of Germany in the years immediately following the war, the military forces and armaments were in excess of the limits fixed by the treaty. In order to face current threats, two subsidiary bodies had been enrolled as well as the *Reichswehr;* one was the security police, the *Sicherheitspolizei,* and the other the *Einwohnerwehr*, a volunteer force of civil guards.

A conference in San Remo in April 1920 received a request from Germany for permission to maintain temporarily an army of 200,000; this was refused. At Boulogne in June 1920, the disbanding of the *Sicherheitspolizei* was demanded; in addition, Germany was reminded to execute the provisions required of her by the treaty. A conference at Spa on 5 June 1920, another in Paris from 24 to 30 January 1921, discussed the matter of German armaments; it acted upon the discussion and received no satisfactory reply from Berlin.

At a London conference, held between 25 February and 14 March 1921, the Allies were determined that the disarmament provisions would be implemented. Germany responded after the occupation of the three German towns. The terms of the ultimatum were accepted: on 19 March the *Reichstag* passed a bill of disarmament in which the

Reichswehr was reduced to 100,000 men. In a note of 29 September, five points were set out to indicate the areas in which compliance with the treaty were still missing. No satisfactory reply was received and the occupation of the Ruhr suspended the work of the IMCC. It was resumed in 1924 when an extended visit of inspection was carried out in a selection of German towns – namely, Rostock, Berlin, Dresden, Stuttgart, Munich, Paderborn, Breslau and Frankfurt-am-Main.

On 8 September 1924, four months before the scheduled evacuation of the first zone (Cologne and surrounding area), the IMCC submitted an interim report: it reckoned that the treaty provisions regarding armaments had still not been fulfilled. On 27 December the Conference of Ambassadors[2] decided 'that the evacuation of Allied troops from Cologne would not begin on 10 January 1925, as scheduled. Thus, the French, supported by the English, Belgians and Italians, made clear their intention to enforce the Versailles Treaty by continued occupation.'[3]

This decision of the Conference of Ambassadors was communicated officially to the German government on 5 January 1925. It had been previously agreed by the Allies that Cologne would only be evacuated if the disarmament inspection carried out by the IMCC proved satisfactory. Stresemann and the German chancellor, Wilhelm Marx, were caught on the horns of a dilemma. They ordered the *Reichswehr* to cooperate with the inspectors, but were met with a refusal.

Stresemann saw one possible compromise, as the price of Cologne, to offer a pact of non-aggression, arbitration and military agreement between 'those powers interested in the Rhine'. This he did with considerable secrecy in January 1925. Lord D'Abernon, who had earlier proposed such a pact, commented in his memoirs:

> There is not the smallest doubt that if the German proposal ... which initiated the official negotiations leading to Locarno, had become known to the public in the early months of the year, all chance of a successful issue would have disappeared … there can be little question that Stresemann would have been turned out of office, and there is a strong possibility that he would have been assassinated.[4]

An account of the Locarno Pact and its effect on German disarmament await the reparations settlement.

Reparations

In December 1922, Charles Evans Hughes, the US secretary of state, made a speech in New York and sketched out a plan to solve the reparations problem.

> If statesmen cannot agree … why should they not invite men of the highest authority in finance in their respective countries – men of such prestige, experience and honour that their agreement upon the amount to be paid and upon a financial plan for working out the payments, would be accepted throughout the world as the most authoritative expression available.[5]

On 13 October 1923 the British government took the initiative to ask the government of the United States whether it were possible to stand by the secretary of state's suggestion; were there American citizens who would be prepared to act? Although membership of the Reparations Commission was refused, an offer of help was made. The result was the establishment of the two subcommittees of experts, already mentioned. The first, headed by the Americans, Brigadier-General Charles Dawes and Owen D. Young, were joined by two members each from Britain, France, Italy and Belgium. The British members were Sir Robert M. Kindersley and Sir Josiah Stamp. The committee was finally constituted on 27 December 1923.

Germany's poor situation in the autumn of 1923 included problems that required immediate action: French troops still occupied the Ruhr; German industry had suffered; the mark had all but collapsed; the *Rentenmark* was in its infancy; Germany owed vast sums to the Allies, which it was unable to repay; and the Allies in turn owed nearly ten billion dollars to the USA.

Meanwhile, Gustav Stresemann had invoked Article 234 of the Treaty of Versailles and had, on 24 October 1923, requested that national experts carry out an investigation into Germany's economic condition and capacity to pay.

The first meetings of the Dawes subcommittee were held in Paris in January 1924; the committee then met in Berlin. On 9 April 1924 a report was made to the Reparations Commission. Its terms of reference had been interpreted widely and covered all the German economic and financial systems and the effect on them of reparation payments.

A new taxation system was planned from which

reparation payments could be met by an eventual annual two-and-a-half million gold marks, obtained from customs duties and customs taxation, from the railways, from transport tax and from industry. Germany would receive a loan from the USA of 800 million gold marks to stimulate its economy. Annual payments by Germany were to start at 1000 million marks for the next five years and thereafter they would rise to 2500 million marks; these were very large sums of money.

The reorganization of the *Reichsbank* was designed and placed under Allied supervision. It was proposed that it should be administered by a general board consisting of 14 members, one half of whom were to be German and the remainder would consist of one each from Britain, France, Italy, Belgium, the United States, Holland and Switzerland. The president of the *Reichsbank* would be a German national. A new set of administrators to effect the proposed reorganization was also put in place.

The German government adopted the Dawes plan on 16 April 1924. The British, Belgian and Italian governments also adopted it; the French lagged behind, but Poincaré was defeated at the French elections in May and was succeeded in office by Monsieur Edouard Herriot. He and Ramsay MacDonald, the British prime minister, met at Chequers on 21 June, when the two socialist prime ministers decided to work for 'a kind of moral pact of cooperation ... for the good of the general interest and of the world'.[6]

At an international reparations conference in London on 16 July 1924, the Dawes Plan was adopted by the representatives of ten nations. France agreed to withdraw its troops from the Ruhr, for which a time limit was set. On 29 August the German government passed the necessary laws through the *Reichstag* for the execution of the Dawes Plan, which came into force on 1 September. It only remained for the Allies to fix the percentage of the reparations payments they would each receive, as German obligations began to roll in.

The operation of the Dawes Plan marked a new period of international relations. Nonetheless, at the same time it was recognized that its terms were inadequate to solve the payment of reparations on a permanent basis. Germany could not continue the large level of annual payments for long and the USA was intent to recover the nearly ten billion dollars that it had loaned to the Allied countries during and immediately after the war. The European nations needed to receive their share of the reparations to repay the debt. The subject of reparations was not just going to go away.

Locarno

Would the evacuation of British troops from Cologne take place according to the time-scale that had been set out by the Treaty of Versailles for the first zone, namely 10 January 1925? With the failure of the Germans to comply with disarmament requirements, it seemed unlikely at the end of 1924. In the middle of December 'Berlin tested Allied willingness to withdraw in spite of the reported lapses in disarmament'.[7] It became clear that France would regard such a move as a breach of military security, which was dependent on two factors: German disarmament and the occupation of the Rhineland; compromise was not possible.

It was at this juncture that Stresemann became aware of a possible Anglo–French pact in the making, and, as has been mentioned before, conceived his own non-aggression mutual guarantee measure. This became known as the Rhineland Pact. He communicated this to London through Lord D'Abernon who, as already stated, had a part in its creation.

Austen Chamberlain, who had been British foreign secretary since November 1924, was suspicious of Stresemann's proposal when it was put before him; he supposed that the evacuation of the entire Rhineland was threatened and that attempts were being made to divide the British from the French. The 'Geneva Protocol' on the peaceful settlement of international disputes through compulsory arbitration, which the British government had previously presented to the League of Nations in October 1924, was discarded by the Conservative government in December. Chamberlain became gradually 'more favourably disposed to the German suggestion'. He was anxious to offer a definite British guarantee to France, but members of the Cabinet did not agree.

Eventually, in March, Chamberlain told the French prime minister, Monsieur Herriot, that a quadrilateral pact, including Germany, 'might be of great assurance to the peace of Europe'. After some unsatisfactory conversations with Herriot in Paris, Chamberlain returned to London to speak with Stanley Baldwin, the British prime minister, who called together a few Cabinet colleagues. Some of these were opposed to the Stresemann plan: Baldwin undertook, as a promise to Chamberlain, to persuade them to change their minds.

On 20 March the British Cabinet agreed to allow Britain to participate in the Rhineland Pact and, on 24 March, Chamberlain announced this decision to parliament. The pact provided for a mutual guarantee of the Franco/German and Belgo/German frontiers by the United Kingdom, Italy and the three powers directly concerned; it also guaranteed the demilitarization of the Rhineland. It was not exactly what Chamberlain had in mind, but it was a step towards European peace before the articles of the Treaty of Versailles became too relaxed and while the Rhineland was still occupied.

Sir Austen Chamberlain, Aristide Briand, the French foreign minister, and Gustav Stresemann all eventuallly received a Nobel Peace Prize, and Chamberlain also received the Order of the Garter. In September 1925 the German government was asked to attend international discussions at Locarno, a small lakeside town in Switzerland, from which the treaty was to take its name. In accepting the invitation, the German ambassador left with Chamberlain a declaration that referred to the evacuation of Cologne and to disarmament, which, unless it were settled before the conclusion of the pact, 'would prejudice its object, namely understanding and conciliation, as faith in it could not be established so long as a large tract of Germany was occupied'. To this declaration[8] the British government replied that, insofar as the withdrawal of troops from the northern zone in Cologne were concerned, the date of the evacuation 'depended solely on the fulfilment of Germany's disarmament obligations'. The

French, Belgian and Italian governments replied in a similar vein.

Discussions between Britain, France, Italy and Germany took place on 12 and 15 October 1925, as planned, at Locarno. Mussolini arrived in a speedboat across the lake. Stresemann at once raised the question of the evacuation of Cologne; German opinion regarded the failure of British troops to leave as a breach of the treaty and as an injustice. Chamberlain and Briand maintained that questions concerning disarmament, evacuation and conditions in the Rhineland 'could not possibly be brought officially into the scope of the conference'; furthermore, 'there could be no bargaining'. Communications with the British and French representatives about the IMCC revealed that six points with regard to German disarmament still remained unsettled; there was also the question of fixed mountings to the guns at Köningsberg, which the German government considered of supreme importance. 'If the view of the IMCC were met on those points, then disarmament would be considered as satisfactorily carried out.'

The discussions were resumed on 15 October. Chamberlain said that he had come to understand Chancellor Hans Luther's position by the time he returned to Germany, but that the points at issue were not small. Aristide Briand came forward with a suggestion that a note should be addressed to the ambassadors' conference to clarify which points with regard to disarmament had been settled and which were still outstanding. Stresemann recognized that the Allies were not prepared to budge and suggested that Germany should give an undertaking that, should the outstanding points be considered met, the

Allies would agree to evacuate Cologne of British troops by a given date. Briand gave such an undertaking.

In the British high commission's report it is commented that 'The German delegation had not done badly. They had been defeated in their attempt to exchange Cologne for Locarno, but they were going to be paid before their job was finished, and they had Monsieur Briand's word that he would support them, even to the sacrifice of his own political position.'

According to the majority of those who attended, the discussions at Locarno provided an occasion for jubilation when significance was accorded to the 'Treaty of Mutual Guarantees'. But there were still plenty of problems, one of which was the immediate future of the British troops in Cologne.

Chapter 7
THE BRITISH ARMY LEAVES COLOGNE FOR WIESBADEN (1926–29)

In accordance with the agreement reached at Locarno on 23 October 1925 the German government presented a note to the Conference of Ambassadors. The note set out those points in the disarmament question that had caused the greatest difficulty. In reply, the Conference of Ambassadors, on 6 November, asked how it was proposed to settle the offending matters, expressing the hope that, if a satisfactory reply were to emerge, it might be possible to begin the evacuation of Cologne on 1 December, the date fixed for the signature of the Locarno Pact.[1]

The German government replied on 11 November, but the French government still was not completely satisfied and 'felt constrained to ask for further enlightenment'. German experts were sent to Paris and, as the result of the negotiations that followed, on 16 November the Conference of Ambassadors was able to tell the German government that the evacuation of the northern zone could start on 1 December and be carried through as quickly as possible.

Those involved in the negotiations commented on the extent to which the Locarno agreement had affected their relationships for the better, especially with the Germans, although this state of affairs was to be of short duration. For the time being, however, replies and assurances came rapidly, though not altogether safely for the Germans, since not all were enthusiastic about the pact. For a start, both the nationalists and the communists were opposed to it. Support from Allied foreign ministers was forthcoming and 'the dangerous moment passed'; on 27 November the *Reichstag* approved the Locarno agreement, though only by a narrow majority.

The War Office needed to decide on a location for the new British zone. Koblenz was thought of as a possibility, but it was rejected on the grounds that it was already the site of the Inter-Allied Rhineland High Commission and also because there was French opposition to relinquishing that area. Wiesbaden was then chosen as the most suitable future home for the British army in Germany. It was agreed that French troops would find space elsewhere in their zone and that the British would occupy the northern portion of what was known as the Mainz bridgehead and a small slip of territory on the left bank of the Rhine, which included the town of Bingen.

Cologne had changed a good deal since it had last been described in 1920. And, who better to give the new account than a journalist and a British officer who were there? In his book entitled *Occupation: 1918–1930: A Postscript to the Western Front,* which has already been mentioned, Ferdinand Tuohy gives his own view of what life in Cologne offered the British army: it was better, he considered, than life in a garrison town elsewhere in places he had known like Aldershot, Egypt and India.

There was still discipline, as well as a lot of training, ceremonial and constantly having to wear a uniform, but there was also plenty of sport. Year after year football leagues 'provoked keen competition'; cricket pitches were made 'on every spare piece of grass that could be found'; and tennis courts were built. Aquatic sports took place in various baths in Cologne and each year a great swimming gala was organized at Poll on the Rhine. An 18-hole golf course was constructed at Rodenkirchen and a Cologne gymkhana club held five or six race meetings a year on the Merheim race course.

The British army developed its own shops, cafés, theatres and clubs. Seats for British nationals would be reserved at the opera and plays, ranging from Shakespeare classics to more contemporary topical productions, were performed at a British playhouse called the Deutsches Theatre, at which many celebrated artists from Britain appeared.

Robert Coulson was posted to Cologne as a regimental officer just after Christmas 1922. His mother came from the Rhineland and, since he was bilingual, he was able to visit his German relations and speak their language fluently.

His book, *The Uneasy Triangle,* written under the pseudonym 'Apex' and based on his time in Germany shortly after the end of the First World War, was intended to encompass the three nations, Britain, France and Germany. A few years ago I was able to engage in a short correspondence with him, then aged 96, just before his death. During a second tour of duty in Cologne he was appointed for special duties in a new department, acting as a link between GHQ and the German administration.

With his perfect knowledge of German, he was able to converse fluently with a broad spectrum of the population, although at times he chose to adopt an English accent because he thought that it would make him appear less menacing. His accounts of some of these conversations point to one reason why, after so short an interval, a second war was likely to break out. In one outburst of real bitterness, Coulson heard words[2] that were characteristic of certain elements in the population and in the future were to have such a sorry outcome:

> We fought the war to the last ounce of our strength. ... Two million of our men were killed ... women starved and our children developed rickets and became idiots through under-feeding. All that was nothing ... it was the price we paid to win. ...But one thing remains. The other side won and we lost. We paid the price and got nothing for it; worse than nothing, for we were beaten and we got the revolution and inflation. We lost something worse than our children and our money: we held out; we bore everything during the war because we

> believed without doubt that we were on the just side; on God's side, as we were told constantly by the Church and the government, yet we were beaten hopelessly.
>
> You can imagine perhaps what it means to lose money, territories, power and prestige. But no one who has not been through the experience could realize the paralysing disillusionment of defeat.

It would seem that the private soldiers and NCOs of the British Rhine army enjoyed their sojourn in Germany more than the officers did. The former were more welcome in German homes of an equivalent strata of society than the officers were because the German 'official' class kept its distance from the occupiers. Once fraternization had been declared permissible, British soldiers began to marry German women. My father's driver in Wiesbaden, whose name was Goddard, was one such person. Originally a British soldier, he had married a German woman, had two children and opted to remain in Germany as a civilian when his unit returned to England. This was not unusual and approximately a hundred English firms were established locally.

In November 1999 Professor Richard Holmes, the military historian, brought together some very old former members of the British Army of the Rhine in a radio programme on the BBC and I was invited to join them. Professor Holmes described the occupation as an event right on the edge of living memory and one of the forgotten stories of the twentieth century. The old soldiers spoke of their good experiences of meeting members of the population of Cologne: Gunner Arthur Whitlock RA, aged 108, was at the time of the programme the oldest man in England. Private Stan Clayton, then aged 105, spoke of the happy Christmas he had spent with a German family; Private Horace Culvert of the West Yorkshire Regiment thought that British and German people felt sympathy for one another; and Private Frederick Saunders RE, was billeted in a school and sang operatic duets with a schoolmistress.

General Sir William Robertson relinquished his command of the British Army of the Rhine in March 1920 and during the same month Lieutenant-General Sir Thomas Morland, formerly in command of the sixth corps, took over. On his return to England General Robertson was promoted to the rank of field marshal, thereby achieving the aspiration he expressed in the title of his autobiography, *From Private to Field Marshal.*[3] General Morland had previously served in Nigeria. His service in Germany lasted only two years due to his poor health and he subsequently developed tuberculosis. His successor, Lieutenant-General Sir Alexander Godley, GCB, KCMG, whose appointment dated from 8 March 1922, has left an autobiography[4] that records his appreciation of his own service in the Rhineland. The commander-in-chief's house was at Marienburg, a suburb about four miles up the Rhine from Cologne. It had a charming garden, a view over the river and its own landing stage, which allowed guests to arrive by water. He entertained not only members of his own command, but also those of the French, American and Belgian armies.

Despite the early traumatic incidents in connection with

the move of French and Belgian troops into the Ruhr (and with the use of railways through the British zone), Godley's later months were uneventful militarily. James Edmonds, however, records[5] an awkward requirement of having to dispose of 'some four thousand rounds of 4.5-inch howitzer gas shells'. The War Office raised objections to the proposal to dump them in the Rhine and eventually a WD vessel collected them for disposal into the sea. General Godley relinquished his command on 16 June 1924 on his appointment to Aldershot. It was, therefore, his successor, Lieutenant-General Sir John Du Cane KCB,[6] who took the British army to Wiesbaden.

The size of the occupying forces at this stage was given in the British high commission report of 1926 as follows:[7]

Second and third zones (Koblenz and Wiesbaden)

Total number of troops September 1925	70,000
French troops	62,000
Total number of troops June 1926	76,000
French troops	60,000
Belgian troops	7,102
British troops	8,118

The evacuation from Cologne began on 30 November 1925 and was achieved, to everybody's astonishment, by 31 January 1926. The weather was extremely cold, which meant that ice impeded travel by barge on the Rhine. Most of the troops travelled by rail in carriages festooned with icicles. The supply of quarters and other accommodation in Wiesbaden was limited and caused serious problems.

Members of the French army, who had taken possession of most of the available space, were reluctant to move elsewhere. The German press made the most of the fact that some of the accommodation thus relinquished needed to be fumigated. In a well-known Berlin comic paper called *Kladderdatsch,* a cartoon entitled *Interallierter Quartierwechsel in Wiesbaden* (inter-allied exchange of quarters in Wiesbaden) showed a British Colonel Pearsoap, followed by an orderly carrying tennis rackets and footballs, and three cleaning women taking over a grimy billet from 'the French Captain Saligot'. Needless to say, the high commission banned that issue of *Kladderdatsch.*

The departure from Cologne was marked by a ceremony on 30 January in Dom Square, opposite the British army headquarters at the Excelsior Hotel, at 3.00 p.m. Sightseers had been gathering since early morning and the square was crowded. The Union Jack was hauled down, the band played 'God Save the King' and the troops (the second Shropshire Light Infantry) presented arms. The large force of German police on duty saluted and many spectators took off their hats. A loud cheer greeted the lowering of the flag, but it was reported that soldiers of the British army received a friendly farewell and that German families entertained them in cafés.

At midnight on 31 January an official ceremony took place on the steps of the cathedral to celebrate the city's freedom from occupation. Speeches were made by Dr Adenauer, *Oberbürgomeister* of Cologne and Dr Otto Braun, the Prussian prime minister. Dr Adenauer spoke from the steps leading up to the west front of the cathedral.

> Hear me! Cologne is free! The hour so fervently longed for, has come; the day of freedom has dawned. Our hearts rise to God, the Almighty. ... We have had seven long years to bear a heavy burden under the hard fist of the victor. ... We have borne suffering in common. ... Let us swear unity, loyalty to the nation, love to our fatherland. ... Cry with me 'Germany, dearest Fatherland', Hurra, Hurra![8]

But the ceremonies that marked the end of the Cologne occupation were not over. On 21 March 1926 the president, Field Marshal Paul von Hindenburg, paid a formal visit to Cologne. Adenauer made another speech in which he fully expressed his grievances about the experience of occupation.[9] As his biographer declares, 'In that one speech Adenauer managed wholly to destroy his previous reputation with the British for fairness and objectivity.'

The British high commissioner, Lord Kilmarnock, wrote angrily to the Foreign Office and it has been noted that the speech played a part in the events that took place 20 years later. To achieve the simultaneous evacuation of all Allied troops from the Cologne area, the British commander-in-chief was anxious to ensure that the French and Belgian troops who were occupying outlying portions of the northern zone should all leave at the same time. Arrangements were made to enable a small Belgian liquidating force to remain in the zone for a short period only, and this was achieved without too much difficulty. During 1926 the Belgian troops that had been stationed in the Krefeld area withdrew to locations in the vicinity of Aix-la-Chapelle.

The number of British troops to move to Wiesbaden was 7843 (from an establishment of 9197). Units were more scattered than they had been in Cologne and they included members of the King's Dragoon Guards; the 8th Field Brigade RFA; the 7th Field Company R; the 1st Cameron Highlanders; the 2nd Worcestershire Regiment; the 2nd Royal Berkshire Regiment; the 1st Oxfordshire and Buckinghamshire Light Infantry; the 2nd Shropshire Light Infantry; the 1st Royal Ulster Rifles, the 1st Manchester Regiment, together with the Signals, Electrical and Mechanical Section; the Military Police; the Royal Army Medical Corps; the Corps of Royal Engineers; the Royal Army Ordinance Corps; the Royal Army Pay Corps, the Royal Army Service Corps; the Army Educational Corps, the Royal Army Veterinary Corps; the Army Dental Corps; and the army post office and chaplains of the ACD.

At the time of the evacuation of the Cologne zone, the army authorities were irritated by the obstructions encountered from local German administrators. Attacks on the British were also made in articles in the German press. The *Regierungspräsident* of Wiesbaden explained to the British commander-in-chief that the object was to secure a reduction in the number of troops of occupation. It was pointed out that Monsieur Aristide Briand had given assurances to Herr Gustav Stresemann at Locarno that he would consider any increase in the occupation of the second and third zones (namely Koblenz and Wiesbaden) as a consequence of the evacuation of the first, as most unjust.

The German ambassador in London continued to appeal to the British government to exercise pressure on Paris.

Since the British and Belgian contingents that remained on the Rhine were comparatively small, the only force that 'could submit to an appreciable reduction and still preserve homogeneity' was the French one. 'A considerable section of public opinion in France was moving steadily towards the belief that the country had made sufficient gestures of conciliation. The military party declared itself to be definitely opposed to any further weakening of the French garrison on the Rhine.'[10]

Throughout the occupation the French army remained in a state of readiness to defend France from any possible attack by Germany, so hence the perpetual wearing of steel helmets, with the characteristic ridge down the middle, by French soldiers as a sign of 'active service'. Herr Gustav Stresemann told Lord D'Abernon, the British ambassador in Berlin with whom he maintained a close friendship, that if the total number of troops could be got down to 60,000, with a further reduction of 5000 when Germany entered the League of Nations, he thought public opinion would cease to be a source of worry on this point to the German government.

Stresemann made no secret of the fact that he was working towards complete evacuation of foreign troops. Lord D'Abernon's diary, which was published in 1929, showed that as early as 25 January 1923, he was questioning the point of retaining a British military force in the Rhineland.

> My original impression had been that it was desirable to continue the occupation by British troops, but when one comes to consider the argu-

> ments, it is strange how little there is to be said for maintaining them. Until recently one thought that the presence of British troops would exercise a moderating influence, but that mission has more or less failed. If they do not moderate, what do they do? They certainly do not protect, and they absorb money which might go to reparations.

He goes on to maintain 'curiously enough' that the Germans would be averse if the British abandoned their present position: 'It would be worse were the French and Belgians in Koblenz' (he was referring to the American zone). He has pity for both Lord Kilmarnock and General Godley whose position was complicated both by the French move into the Ruhr and the policy of support for the Rhineland as a buffer state. Whether his innate diplomatic sense prevented him from discussing these issues with his friend Herr Stresemann remains conjecture.

Because of a veto by Brazil, Germany was unable to enter the League of Nations in March 1926. In April, a German request for more police in the occupied territories was rejected. The presence of 150,000 German police, armed and trained as soldiers, and under trained officers, was already creating some alarm. James Edmonds[11] provides information that claims that the Reich in 1926 possessed an army of at least 250,000, plus reserves, instead of the 100,000 as required by the peace treaty.

During the summer of 1926 the question of a reduction in the numbers of occupying troops came up again. Monsieur Briand, in his reply to a note he had received from Sir Austen Chamberlain, claimed that whenever he had approached his war ministry to consider the question of reductions, it had pointed to the increasing boldness of the German nationalist associations. Recent incidents (which are dealt with later) had made it difficult to press the matter further. On the other hand, Stresemann gave special instructions to the German authorities in the Rhineland 'to discourage all festivals and demonstrations likely to arouse the susceptibility of the occupying forces'. Efforts were being made to curb the activities of nationalists.

On 16 August 1926, the Foreign Office in London asked the War Office if it would be prepared to make a further reduction in the numbers of the British Army of the Rhine. The War Office replied in the negative. The entry of Germany into the League of Nations took place on 8 September 1926 and, within a week, Monsieur Briand and Dr Stresemann had met in a friendly fashion at Thoiry. But a series of clashes between members of the German population and occupation forces in the French and British zones, in which blood was shed, overshadowed the event.

General Sir John Du Cane, the General Officer Commander-in-Chief of the British Army of the Rhine, resigned in 1927 on becoming governor and commander-in-chief in Malta. His place in Germany was taken by Lieutenant-General Sir William Thwaites KCB, KCMG, who during his career held the post of director of military intelligence at the War Office. It was he who masterminded the evacuation of the British army from the Rhineland in 1929.

Before he did so, he faced a range of different situations that required his intelligence and experience. Excitement was aroused in Berlin in August 1928 when it was announced that the 8th Hussars were intending to participate in the French autumn manoeuvres. The press commented in such a frenzied manner that it caused questions to be asked in the House of Commons. A perfectly reasonable explanation was provided that since there were no facilities at Wiesbaden for training an isolated cavalry regiment, an invitation to join in military exercises under the command of General Guillaumat was gratefully accepted.

Probably encouraged by their areas having become so close, relations between the British and French commanders became particularly cordial during the Wiesbaden era and this marked an improvement in British–French relations in general. In past years the tensions between them had been frequent. General Thwaites emphasized this good relationship in his report.[12] He was customarily invited to stand beside the French commander on ceremonial occasions (such as the parade of French troops on 14 July), and he would return the compliment during the King's birthday celebrations.

Relationships with the Belgian general commanding the Belgian army on the Rhine at Aix-la-Chapelle were also friendly, with visits being paid to each other every six months or so. However, a crisis arose on Armistice Day 1928 because it fell on a Sunday and thus interfered with the customary use of German churches: nationalists protested in the *Reichstag* and the German commissioner raised the matter because if British troops were to attend at 11.00 a.m. it would deprive German congregations of their normal facilities for worship.

A good deal of friction followed, particularly when the

clock on the Ringkirche (a church in Wiesbaden) was prevented from striking for two hours, namely from 10.00 a.m. to midday. The suggestion was made that the British army had been 'guilty of [a] despotic demonstration of triumph'.[13] Against this insinuation, the British high commissioner had protested that Armistice Day was supposed to be a thanksgiving for the re-establishment of peace and a commemoration of the fallen, in whose memory the two-minute silence was a solemn tribute.

The winter of 1928/9 was exceptionally severe, much colder than normally experienced. The hard weather began during the second week of December 1928 and continued without respite until the first week of March 1929. The Rhine river was completely frozen over and, at some points, the ice was three feet thick; shipping was brought to a standstill. In his report on the period from a military point of view, General Thwaites commented on the 'special care' that was required to be taken of the troops on fatigues and sentry and guard duty. Protective clothing was issued in the form of fur-lined mittens, hats and coats to be worn over army greatcoats. Lighted braziers were provided for sentries and duties were reduced to one hour in length. General Thwaites revealed that French soldiers were less fortunate and suffered considerable casualties, with some even being frozen to death, through a lack of precautions. General Guillaumat, who had hitherto enjoyed a blameless reputation, was severely criticized over this episode.

Chapter 8
THE INTER-ALLIED RHINELAND HIGH COMMISSION

Another set of foreign occupiers in the 1920s Rhineland were the British, French and Belgian civilians who were part of the Inter-Allied Rhineland High Commission (IARHC) in the town of Koblenz, my birthplace and home for the first seven-and-a-half years of my life. A sympathetic view of Koblenz has been written in *Tides and Eddies*[1] by the sister of Lieutenant-Colonel Rupert Ryan, who was deputy British high commissioner from 1920 to 1929. She was always known as Maie Ryan, although her real names were Ethel Marian.[2]

> Koblenz was smaller, more intimate than the great city of Cologne. Built on the northern tip of a peninsular created by the break-away of the river

> Mosel from the west bank of the parent Rhine, the city was supported and softened by the woods behind it that sank steeply towards the Mosel. Between the high bulk of Ehrenbreitstein and the river Lahn, lay another sweep of woods - lands rising and falling into waves. These rises were a feature of the banks of the Rhine as far north as Bonn; they concealed villages that came suddenly to life at certain times of the year when bonfires were lit at the highest points to celebrate the Catholic festivals. ... The countryside showed an ordered beauty under the snow of winter as in the thick green of summer.

For us it became filled with romance through the history of its people and the legendary beings who were their companions and creations in the forest or on the islands and rocks of the Rhine. Even the deer and boar that lived in the woods seemed to belong to a fairy tale.

The Inter-Allied Rhineland High Commission, as the supreme authority of the occupation, can best be examined from two angles: first, its function and its staff in three nationalities; second, the families of this staff living in requisitioned accommodation throughout Koblenz and among the German population. It was with these families that I was to be particularly associated.

A part of the Treaty of Versailles called the Rhineland Agreement spelt out how the civilian body, the IARHC, was called to oversee the military regimes in the occupied zones. As already described in the Introduction, the local Rhineland authorities retained their civil administration under German law and were subject to a central German government, except over 'The Armed forces of occupation and the persons accompanying them' who were 'exclusively subject to the military law and jurisdiction of such forces'. The work of the local court remained intact, but the IARHC could transfer cases from them if it were thought necessary in the interests of the security or dignity of the force concerned.

The high commission operated by issuing ordinances and any offences against these ordinances were made amenable to military jurisdiction. It was left 'to the discretion of the Commander-in-Chief of the individual army' to decide what method to employ in the exercise of this jurisdiction. Summary courts were set up in each zone of occupation and the law of the army concerned would determine what procedure would prevail. This led to very dissimilar practices being employed in neighbouring zones.

The British summary court was conducted along the lines of a magistrate's court in England and it was presided over by a barrister-at-law. After the move to Wiesbaden, Major H. Gatehouse began to sit there on 12 January 1926. A permanent prosecutor, who was another barrister-at-law, was also appointed. The application of British law was consequently carried on with full justice. The commander-in-chief had power, in serious cases, to arraign a special military court conducted along the lines of a general court martial, but only two of these courts were convened during the Wiesbaden period.

The British summary court at Cologne heard 3700 cases between 1919 and 1925 and another 595 at Wiesbaden between 1926 and 1929. These cases tended to be about matters such as the illegal possession of arms, entering carriages reserved for officers, being on British premises without authority, being in possession of British government property, and reckless driving. The sentences were often fines and any custodial sentences, which ranged from seven to fourteen days, were served in German prisons.

The Germans took great interest in the proceedings of the summary court and would attend all the sittings in large numbers in the section of the court reserved for the public. German lawyers made a practice of attending in order to study British procedure and methods.

During the 12 years of occupation, the high commission issued 312 ordinances, all of which were backed by the force of law and were required to be carried out by military and civilian bodies. Some caused a good deal of disturbance among the German population, particularly those that were to do with domestic matters: these included the absolute control of the local press; censorship of plays, books and films (all in all some 40 films were banned, mostly in the French zone). The flying of national flags was banned, as also was the playing of nationalistic music; also prohibited were the wearing of uniforms, membership of certain societies and the licensing of 'spirituous liquors'.

The function of the high commission

The banning of relatively trivial activities, considered by the Germans as threats to their liberty, could lead to serious demonstrations. After Locarno, attempts were made to take a more lenient view of German actions and not automatically to impose widespread ordinances. Examples follow of events in the occupied territories in 1926 where insurrections were stirred up by minor incidents. One was the illumination of the Niederwald-denkmal monument on 7 May 1926. The high commission learnt that to celebrate the visit of the German board of agriculture to Bingen on 8 May, the local German authorities proposed to illuminate the Niederwald-denkmal, generally known as 'Germania', which stands on the hills behind Rüdesheim. The monument, made of captured French cannon, was erected to celebrate the German victories in the war of 1870/1.

The names of Sedan and others were inscribed on its base. To French sensibilities, this proposal could be considered inflammatory. General Guillaumat, the French commander who took over from General Degoutte, regarded the suggestion as a substantial provocation on the German part and asked the high commission to ban the illumination.

Due mainly to the inefficiency of the German commissioner at the IARHC to prevent this occurrence, however, it took place as arranged. The British high commission report for 1926 comments that, 'seized upon by the German and French Press, this incident received an importance and evoked an outcry, which was both exaggerated and undesirable.'

In the garrison town of Germersheim, with a population of 3000 inhabitants, almost the same number of French troops were in occupation. On 3 and 4 July 1926 the

8. General Adolphe Guillaumat.

townspeople arranged to hold a festival of the *Germersheimer Krieger und Veteranen Verein* at which 86 ex-servicemen's associations were represented. The total number of participants was about 2500, most of whom were strangers to the town, and lavish decorations abounded. Flagpoles were erected, the old national colours were flown everywhere and the windows of the houses bore bunting and festoons.

The local German authorities decided to adopt the view

that, since it was not a political festival, it was not incumbent upon them to notify the occupying authorities. In fact, the French army did not even know about the fête until the morning of 3 July.

On the afternoon of 4 July, a procession of veteran associations marched round the town carrying 86 banners or flags bearing the names of the victories of 1870. *Deutschland über Alles* and *Siegreich wollen wir Frankreich schlagen*[3] were played during the march.

The occupying troops reacted violently and there were a number of incidents in which flags were removed or trodden underfoot. In fact, during the festival a great number of flags and flagmasts were torn down. Since the occupying authorities were of the view that as long as strict ordinances were in place there would be fewer incidents, a return to these controls was advised.

Paul Tirard, the French high commissioner, wrote[4] that processions and demonstrations were an outward sign of the gregarious instincts that, for ages past, had characterized the German race. In no country other than Germany was the right of association regarded as a natural right to be jealously defended and exercised. The occupying authorities respected this, with two exceptions: first, any association that engaged in military training, the use of arms or preparation for war in one form or another was formally forbidden; and second, any group that upheld sentiments that were hostile to the Allied authorities, or that organized plots against the rulers, were also forbidden. In practice, however, it was extremely difficult to control these associations because they used subterfuge to escape detection.

As an example, Monsieur Tirard wrote about the *Reitervereine* the authorities noticed were appearing simultaneously in all the towns and villages of the Rhineland. These groups of cavalry were officially show riders, but they bore all the hallmarks of preparing for military engagement. As a result of official protestations, the organization hurriedly removed from its ranks any members that were liable to criticism, and diverted them into agricultural activities geared towards improving the breeding of horses. But ex-cavalry officers remained in the *Reitervereine* and continued to teach military drill. The British high commission report for 1927 gave the figures for *Reitervereine* in the occupied territories in March of that year as 100 clubs with a total membership of 5000. Other associations with sinister connotations will be discussed in Chapter 9.

Unfortunately, the nationalist press painted the French role in the Germersheim action in its worst colours; diplomatic efforts to bury the whole matter as quietly as possible became difficult. A commission of inquiry on inter-Allied lines was suggested by the German commissioner, but before any action was taken, there was an incident in Koblenz on 13 July in connection with the celebration of the French national day: a German brass band started up just as the French procession was passing and the Germans booed and hissed. About 500 East Prussians, well known for their nationalistic tendencies, had taken part. German official apologies were made to the French military headquarters.

The affair at Germersheim was not so easily settled. The British government, when approached, strongly advised the German authorities to drop any action that would only prolong and intensify animosity. Dr Stresemann again applied his diplomatic and conciliatory attitude and stressed that steps that had been taken to reduce the reintroduction of repressive legislative should not be rescinded.

Other incidents took place in 1926. At Trier four bicyclists, three of whom were German and the fourth a Frenchman employed in the garrison pharmacy, collided with a small group of pedestrians on 26 September. A violent argument ensued during which the Frenchman drew out a revolver and fired several shots, one of which killed a German. At a military court the assailant claimed that he was acting in self-defence and received a suspended sentence of six months' imprisonment. A few days later at Neustadt, a French sergeant sitting in a café was approached by a German of known nationalist sentiments who drunkenly invited him to join him for a drink. On his refusal, the Frenchman was stabbed under the heart and his assailant made off on a motorcycle.

On 26 September a new conflict broke out at Germersheim when a group of Germans threatened a French lieutenant by the name of Rouzier for misbehaving with German women. The French officer fired his revolver, killed one German and wounded two others. A French military court acquitted Rouzier and sentenced six Germans to terms of imprisonment ranging from two years to two months. Later Monsieur Briand persuaded the French president to pardon the six condemned Germans by a presidential decree that was signed on Christmas day.

The year was not to close before another incident laid

bare the tensions that existed. On Christmas day 1926 three British soldiers, who had recently arrived in Germany, were thrown out of a café in Idstein and four Germans were, in consequence, charged with their assault at the summary court in Wiesbaden. The prosecution admitted the soldiers had been aggressive, but there was too little evidence to secure a conviction. The case was predictably reported in the German press, which referred 'in a pointed manner to the impartiality and humanity shown by the British court [in the occupied territories] in comparison with the narrow national spirit and war mentality displayed by their French counterparts'.[5]

German requests for a reduction in the number of occupying troops met with some success. During October and November 1926, the French garrison at Andernach was decreased, and those at Kreuznach and Kaiserlauten were each reduced by a battalion of infantry. This had made it possible for the French commander-in-chief to restore three schools and other buildings to the German authorities and, in addition, an aviation ground had been freed and the area could now be used for the sowing of crops.

Dr Stresemann showed his eagerness to create a better atmosphere by exerting his influence on the administrative chiefs of the occupied provinces. He made it clear that, unlike the nationalists, he considered that a popular movement in the Rhineland was a wrong card to play. Rather, it was important to convince the occupiers that Germany intended to comply with the Treaty of Locarno obligations.

The German attempts to secure a reduction in and

withdrawal of foreign troops took various forms. As a prelude to the year 1927, the German commissioner to the IARHC handed in a long list of mostly minor transgressions by British soldiers. In the high commission's reply it was pointed out that the incidents were fewer than among the ordinary civilian population and that if the prominence given to these minor breaches of behaviour was in order to hasten evacuation, it was considered unlikely to succeed.

The only disturbance early in 1927 was instigated by the extreme right-wing nationalists. On 12 February they planned to commemorate the successful storming by nationalists, in 1924, of the separatists' headquarters at Pirmasens. However, the high commission forbade the demonstration and local German police carried out their duties 'with absolute correctness'. Throughout 1927, the German authorities did not intend to allow the evacuation question to be forgotten. In fact, Herr Stresemann went so far as to announce that the lack of progress over the Rhineland question was giving his opponents such a powerful weapon to use against him that he was very seriously considering resignation.

As part of the international picture, early in the year 1927 Sir Austen Chamberlain, the British foreign secretary, related to the German ambassador a remark he had made to the Belgian ambassador a few days earlier. This was that a large section of German opinion seemed to believe that concessions were to be won 'by storm and bluster, rather than genial sunshine'.

On the occasion of the visit of the president of the French Republic, Monsieur Gaston Doumergue, to London on 18 May, Sir Austen Chamberlain and Monsieur Briand, who was at that time the French foreign minister, had an opportunity to discuss the matter of the number of troops in the Rhineland. Briand complained that German methods of propaganda and diplomacy made the French course a difficult one, though a reduction of between 2000 and 3000 men and the liberation of a number of billets had been made.

Constitution Day was due to be celebrated in the occupied territories in August 1927. In Wiesbaden the Republican Reichsbanner Association applied for permission to organize a procession on 10 August. This was granted subject to the restriction that there should be no marching in military formation and no playing of military marches. It was also agreed that a *Windjacke* might be worn, but not 'Sam Brown' belts. These conditions were not observed. Several men wore cross belts, the procession marched in military formation and military marches were played. The British Army authorities prosecuted the organizers of the demonstration and they were each fined 200 marks.

Permission was asked for and granted on 28 August for a *Reichsbanner* demonstration at Rüdesheim. This passed off without incident, although one speaker was reported to have said what amounted to 'We must get rid of the occupation, for we who are Germans cannot do what we wish in our own country.'

An incident in the latter part of 1927 arose over the German Scientific Aviation Society (*Wissenschafliche Gesellschaft für Luftfahrt*) congress at Wiesbaden. Permission was requested for two German officers of the

Reichswehr to be allowed to enter the occupied territory to attend the conference, which was due to be held between 16 and 19 September. The names of the officers were rather suspect: one was reported to have been responsible for coordinating the work of various patriotic organizations; and the other, according to a reliable source, had recently presided at a meeting to discuss a *Reichswehr* ministry plan to extend the German army.

General Thwaites, the British commander-general, was of the opinion that there were ulterior motives behind the request and advised the IARHC to refuse entry to these officers. Why, it was asked, did a town in the occupied territories come to be chosen for the congress? The action caused resentment and the Scientific Aviation Society maintained that the progress of scientific aeronautics was the sole object of the congress. The occupying authorities regarded this as unlikely because the political complexion of the society was definitely nationalistic.

A speech by President Hindenburg at the inauguration of a memorial at Tannenberg on 18 September was reported with exhilaration in the German press because he maintained that Germany was free of war guilt. The speech was answered by Monsieur Barthou on behalf of France and, with some bitterness, by Monsieur Jaspar on behalf of Belgium. At Geneva, Dr Stresemann supported the president, though with a degree of mitigation in that he claimed that Germany was not solely responsible for the war. The French press made full use of the president's words, particularly in the regions where the war had caused the most devastation.

The general officer commanding the British Army of the

Rhine had given specific instructions that on no account must the total strength under his command exceed 6250. On 1 December 1927 the strength of the French troops was 47,896 (the maximum was 48,500) and that of the Belgians on 10 January, 4712 (instead of 5300). These reductions resulted in the departure of the garrisons of Geilenkirchen and Lendern in the Belgian zone, of Idstein in the British zone and of Dietz and Pfeifflingheim in the French zone. Important reductions also took place in other garrison towns, notably Königstein and Wiesbaden in the British zone, and Düren, Euskirchen, Koblenz and Germersheim in the French zone.

The German commissioner had made a complaint to the high commission that the number of visitors to the watering places in the occupied territories had been reduced as a consequence of occupation. Figures consequently revealed that the number of visitors to the spas had been greatly in excess of any figure since 1914. Wiesbaden had attracted 80,000 tourists up to 27 July 1927. In Koblenz visitors showed an increase of 60 per cent over 1926.

Towards the end of 1928, as a result of meetings between Sir Austen Chamberlain and various foreign statesmen and ambassadors, he came to the conclusion that 'premature evacuation' (that is before 1935) of troops from the Rhineland could not be discussed seriously until the German government had produced an acceptable timetable for the final settlement of Germany's reparations obligations. The sum theoretically and legally due from Germany remained at 132 milliards of gold marks.

An initiative on this matter came from the United States.

The agent general for reparations, Seymour Parker Gilbert, felt that the Germans were borrowing far too much money for their reparation payment. The French government, linking reparations to security, war debt and the maintenance of troops in the Rhineland, agreed to a conference under the chairmanship of Owen D. Young, chairman of the American General Electric Company. The preliminary hearing took place in Paris in February 1929.

An idealistic effort to renounce war as a means of solving international problems came with the signing of the Kellogg Peace Plan with (initially) 15 powers, including Germany, on 27 August 1928. No means were provided for its enforcement. It grew out of a proposal from Monsieur Briand to the United States that America and Germany should mutually outlaw war with one another. Endorsement came from Frank B. Kellogg, the US secretary of state, who gave his name to the pact, though American sources maintain that lesser persons were chiefly responsible.

The matter of the Rhineland, needless to say, was raised privately during the Paris meeting and also at the September meeting of the League of Nations, during which a report arrived to the effect that Dr Stresemann was seriously ill. He had, however, recovered sufficiently to take part in the December meeting of the council of the League of Nations at Lugano. An agreement was reached to persuade the committee of financial experts to begin discussions, through diplomatic channels, on the withdrawal of troops from the Rhineland.

Within the occupied territories a few incidents in 1928 caused the high commission to worry. During January the high commission attracted attention by forbidding, in the interests of public order, two well-known German generals to give lectures in the Palatinate. One of the lectures, given outside the occupied zone, was reported to have been extremely nationalistic in tone. The other, again given in unoccupied Germany and under the title of 'The Defence of German East Africa against the British 1914–18' was enthusiastically received and therefore created some difficulties for the authorities.

The citizens of the high commission

Three high commissioners dominated the Inter-Allied Rhineland High Commission. First among them, and not only in seniority, was without doubt the despotic Paul Tirard, who was its president for the whole life of the commission. Lord Kilmarnock who had succeeded his father as Earl of Erroll on 8 January 1927, and who had been British high commissioner since December 1920, died suddenly of a heart attack on the night of 20 February 1928 in his home in Koblenz. Since he had been born in 1876, he was a mere 52 years of age. The Belgian high commissioners changed more frequently than their colleagues from other nationalities. When the Baron Rolin Jacquemyns resigned in July 1925, Monsieur Forthomme held the appointment from 1926 until Monsieur Le Jeune de Münsbach took over on 4 March 1929.

The arrangements for Lord Erroll's funeral gave rise to problems that were not uncommon in territories occupied by more than one army. General Thwaites wrote in his report[6] that General Guillaumat, the general officer com-

9. Lord Erroll (formerly Lord Kilmarnock), British high commissioner, with Lady Erroll and guard provided by the 2nd battalion of the Royal Fusiliers, Koblenz 1928.

manding the Allied armies, was anxious to parade the French 30 Corps at Koblenz on this occasion, so suddenly took the funeral arrangements in hand without reference to the British general. Fortunately, at a personal interview between the two men, arrangements were amicably adjusted.

The French 30 Corps, under General Guillaumat's orders, lined the streets between the church and the cemetery. Under General Thwaites's orders came the coffin on a British gun carriage; eight pall bearers included the French and Belgian high commissioners, the two generals already mentioned and the commander-in-chief of the Belgian army on the Rhine. The funeral cortège consisted of three companies, Belgian, British and French, with a British band. A battalion of the Royal Artillery then fired a 17-gun salute as the cortège moved through the town.

Lord Erroll had been a popular high commissioner, with a talent for writing plays, two of which were performed in London. Amateur dramatics, with a cast from the British community, took place in the high commissioner's large house along the Rheinanlagen beside the river. Among other events, there were ceremonies on Armistice Day each year, which I remember well; soldiers in uniform included members of the high commissioner's guard provided by the second battalion of the Royal Fusiliers, along with its bugler.

Maie Casey in her book, *Tides and Eddies*, writes of the Erroll's' three children, two of whose lives seemed to go adrift: the eldest, Joss, who was handsome and dashing with a future ahead of him in the Foreign Office, left England for Kenya after having eloped with Lady Idina Gordon, who was twice divorced and nine years older than he. They parted in 1928 and in 1930 he remarried in Kenya's notorious Happy Valley. In 1941 he was found murdered in his Buick at a crossroads in the countryside. The trial, which received a considerable amount of attention, ended with the acquittal of the chief suspect. Joss Erroll's only child, a daughter, became Countess of Erroll.

Joss's sister, Lady Rosemary Hay, then aged 17, came out to Koblenz in 1921 to join her parents. Maie Casey wrote that, 'Like her brother, she could be *un enfant terrible.*' Rosemary attached herself to Lieutenant-Colonel Rupert Ryan, the deputy British high commissioner who was 19 years her senior. 'He tried to resist marriage', wrote his sister Maie, 'but Rosemary's mind was set upon it.' The wedding took place in 1924, but the marriage did not survive for long.

Lord Erroll was succeeded as British high commissioner in the Rhineland in May 1928 by Mr William Seeds who had served in the Foreign Office in South America and was currently British minister in Durazzo (Albania).

The very large former headquarters of the Rhineland province, the *Oberpräsidium* in Clemensplatz, was not only Monsieur Tirard's home, but it also contained the offices of the three high commissioners and their staffs. During the years 1924 to 1928, the British 'officials' numbered about 20, with an additional 29 men and women who served as secretaries, clerks, messengers and drivers. According to the catalogue of passes issued to British personnel and their families, most of the British members of staff were married, so the total British contingent amounted to almost a hundred. This picture would be repeated in the French and Belgian departments. Official receptions and private hospitality took place between those in Allied circles, but there was almost no contact with those of German nationality.

The staff of the IARHC were placed in requisitioned flats and houses throughout Koblenz. During my early childhood, my parents and I lived in a flat in the Rheinzoll Strasse, overlooking the Rhine and the castle of Ehrenbreitstein; later we lived in the Luizen Weg, which was a short road leading to the river. During three months in 1923, my father was required to investigate German army records that were held in Potsdam, so my parents, my German Nanny, Schwester Emmi Baum, and I moved to a hotel in Charlottenburg in Berlin.

10. Members of the Inter-Allied Rhineland High Commission at Koblenz, 1929. Monsieur Tirard, the French high commissioner, is in the centre, Monsieur Forthomme, the Belgian high commissioner, is on the left, and Mr William Seeds, the British high commissioner is on the right. (His successor, Mr James Herbertson, is one from the end on the right.)

Anticipating the birth of my sister Pamela in August 1924, my parents and I moved to a moderately large house with a good garden on Oberwerth, an island in the Rhine reached by a small bridge from the city of Koblenz. A French family relinquished the house for our use and it had to be fumigated because chickens had been accommodated in the attic. There we lived for the next five years until we moved to Wiesbaden when the IARHC went there in the autumn of 1929.

My sister and I did not attend a German school, but a Fröbel-trained governess, Fräulein Lotte Nieburgh, moved in to provide us with daily lessons. She taught us entirely in German (which became extremely useful during the Second World War). She was particularly accomplished in handwork, as well as more academic subjects. I learnt to sew, for which I am eternally grateful; some small cloths, embroidered for my mother in cross stitch, are still in my possession.

In the afternoons, we would go for walks either to castles and ruins with which Koblenz was well endowed, or along the Rhine gardens to the *Deutsches Eck,* the confluence of the Rhine and the Mosel rivers, with the large and imposing statue of Kaiser Wilhelm I on horseback. Our minds were filled with romantic narratives and fed on fairy stories, the works of the Brothers Grimm and Hans Anderson. As a result our games relied a good deal on our imaginations.

We received some books in English from our Scottish aunts, one of whom was a writer of children's works, so our reading matter did include some books in our native tongue, but not to the same extent as it would have had we lived in England.

My sister and I spoke German to each other, to our governess, to our cook and to any other domestic helper. My sister, aged five, could manage simultaneous translations between any of the above and our mother, for whom German remained somewhat elusive. Our mother, in her turn, pulled us up when our English pronunciation was at fault. Our only outside exposure to German people was occasional shopping expeditions in Koblenz with our mother.

Even then shopping for wine was never in German

11. The author with her younger sister and German governess, Koblenz, 1927.

shops, but there were exciting expeditions to the canteen of the French army.

A long low hut gave entry to rows of trestle tables

covered in bottles of French wine. I shall remember for ever the smell of straw with which the bottles were wrapped. We would be served by French *poilu*s in their light-blue uniforms. Delivery was by French military truck.

If we were ill, Dr Bloch would come to see us. Long after we had left Germany and the Nazis were in power, he ran into trouble for, as it was stated, '*Seine Grossmutter war nicht in ordnung*', which meant that she (namely his grandmother) was Jewish. My father made several visits to the Home Office to try to obtain a visa for Dr Bloch to leave Germany for the United States, but he was unsuccessful before the outbreak of the war. Dr Bloch managed to avoid a concentration camp; we heard that he had died in Koblenz just after the war was over.

Our parents entertained a good deal, so my sister and I received a number of toys as presents. My father asked us before each Christmas to give up those that had already given us pleasure. He put them in a sack and made a journey over the Mosel bridge to Koblenz Lützel, a poor industrial area. There he would give the toys to mothers whose children had none of their own. He became legendary as 'the tall *Engländer*' and when he told them in 1929 that we were about to leave Koblenz, several of the women wept.

Communication with Schwester Emmi and Lotte Nieburgh, later Steinicke, ceased with the war, but we made visits some years later to them both; Schwester Emmi made her only visit to England in the 1970s, to see my family, 50 years after she had first joined us in Germany. When we moved from Koblenz to Wiesbaden in

1929, our dog Billy, a rough-haired fox terrier of impeccable British stock, needed to be left behind. He was given to Schwester Emmi, who bred from him; one of the puppies, called by my name, was my legacy to the Rhineland.

The high commission in the year 1929

The year 1929 was dominated by four major happenings, three of which were on the continent and one in England. On the continent the committee of experts, under the chairmanship of Owen D. Young, had struggled to regulate the matter of reparations to be paid by Germany. The new plan, having been initiated by Seymour Parker Gilbert (the agent general of reparations questions) but carrying Young's name, was discussed at the meeting of the Paris Conference in June; it was implemented by the first conference at The Hague in August. Representatives from France, Belgium, Great Britain, Italy and Japan were present. The second happening was the decision made for the premature evacuation of the Rhineland by Allied troops; British and Belgian armies would leave before the end of the current year and the French army by 30 June 1930.

In England, at the general election of 30 May 1929, the Labour Party, for the first time, became the largest party in the House of Commons. On 5 June, James Ramsay MacDonald became prime minister and Arthur Henderson foreign secretary. Labour Party policy, already proclaimed, was to withdraw British troops from the Rhine. Henderson made his first speech in the House of Commons on 5 July, to the effect that: 'It is of the greatest importance that we should make it unmistakably clear that we are anxious that this [the evacuation of the Rhineland] should take place at the earliest possible moment.'

In France there was also a change of prime minister. Raymond Poincaré resigned on 25 July 1929, on grounds of ill health, and Aristide Briand took his place at the end of the month. The final negotiations for the withdrawal from the Rhineland were concluded with him on the French side. Briand became known as the 'apostle of peace' and an advocate of Franco–German reconciliation.

The first conference at The Hague opened on 5 August (after the French had refused to meet in London) and it was convened with a view to completing the discussion about the Young Plan. On 21 June the British ambassador in Paris had been instructed to remind Monsieur Poincaré (who was on 29 June to relinquish the office of prime minister) that Britain maintained the right to take any steps 'they might deem desirable with regard to evacuation without connecting it with any other topic'.[7]

The German government found it acceptable that the Young Plan should be the basis for the conference but only on the understanding that 'other questions raised by the World War' were also permanently settled. The German ambassador called at the Foreign Office and left an *aide-mémoire* setting out the opinion of the German government; the conference scheduled to meet to enforce the Young Plan should consider also the question of the evacuation of the Rhineland. He was informed that the subject would be on the programme.

Two committees were set up at The Hague conference:

there was a financial committee under Belgian chairmanship, of which Philip Snowden, the British chancellor of the exchequer was a member, and there was a committee to discuss political issues, of which Arthur Henderson, the British foreign secretary, was chairman. According to the British high commission report,[8] Snowden had the more difficult assignment, which 'bristled with obstacles'. The subject at issue was the Young Plan for the more expedient payment of reparations. For a month he worked tirelessly for a settlement between the powers. At last agreement was reached and the matter of reparations was eventually settled. Total reparations were set at 26,350 million dollars to be paid over a period of 58½ years. The annual payment of about 473 million was set into two elements, an unconditional part (one-third of the sum) and a postponable part (the remainder).

The political committee could now produce its report; essentially, this was that France, Belgium and Britain had agreed to begin the evacuation of the Rhineland in September and that within three months of the beginning of this period all British and Belgian troops would be completely withdrawn. The French army declined to leave in winter (though the British army was willing to do so across the Channel). The French Prime Minister, Monsieur Briand, gave an assurance that the French army would be out of the Rhineland by 30 June 1930.

An agreement was also reached that Germany would waive claims and occupation costs that arose after 1 September. A special fund was set up to pay for the costs of the occupation armies after that date. It was agreed that a reserve fund of 60 million Reichmarks would be created.

The German government was to contribute 30 million and the occupying powers would make contributions in the following proportions - France 35 per cent, Britain 12 per cent and Belgium 3 per cent.

Outstanding measures needed to be taken in connection with the demilitarization of the Rhineland. At the Geneva meeting of the League of Nations, Monsieur Massigli of the Quai d'Orsay (the French Foreign Office) suggested that the outstanding points should be settled between the German government and military experts at Berlin. So, for the second conference, which was held at The Hague between 3 and 20 January 1930, this matter was included on the agenda.

On 3 October 1929 Dr Stresemann died at 5.25 in the morning. He had been ill for some years, had needed to rest for much of 1928, and had returned to several spas for treatment, but, great German patriot that he was, he refused to give up and his death came after a long day of work. British opinion of him was more consistently favourable than in some quarters of his own country. Lord D'Abernon, during his service as British ambassador in Berlin, wrote of Stresemann that he was 'brilliant, daring and bold. In both [there was] more than a dash of recklessness'.[9] His essential policy, he considered, was to bring about 'such a moderation of hostility between France and Germany as would permit European pacification. To rid Germany of the foreign troops poised on the Rhine was his constant preoccupation. At least it was agreed, even if not achieved, by the time of his death.' From the German point of view, Lord D'Abernon wrote that 'His capacity for arousing animosity was quite outstanding.'[10]

In James Lees-Milne's biography,[11] Harold Nicolson says of Stresemann: 'What a man he was! He managed to combine the convivial with the authoritative, the humorous with the powerful.' Nicolson also recalls 'the howls of execration as Stresemann mounted the tribune of the *Reichstag*'. His biographer comments, on the other hand, 'with Stresemann's departure went the last hope of the Weimar Republic'. Its fragmentary nature, multiplicity of parties and now lack of strong leadership laid it open to dictatorship when this came. Once the evacuation of the Rhineland had become a reality, Stresemann had intended to recover his health with a visit to Egypt and thereafter return to Germany to take part in the elections for the *Reich* presidency in 1932. He would have been an opponent to Hitler; the outcome remains an enigma.

Chapter 9

THE DEVELOPMENT OF NATIONALISTIC SOCIETIES (1929–30)

The emergence of right-wing movements in Germany in the 1920s has already been mentioned, in some cases by name. At first ridiculed or ignored by many, they were to lead to threats to the peace of Europe. Adolf Hitler's Bavarian *putsch* of 1923 was originally looked upon more as a pathetic failure than the beginnings of a serious menace. In the early 1920s the presence of other somewhat similar right-wing organizations thrown up by the high level of unemployment, and by the general social and economic malaise, disguised the particular potential danger of the *National Sozialistsche Deutsche Arbeiterpartei.* It is inappropriate here to provide a history of the development of the movement, but some mention needs to be made of its bearing on the history of the Allied occupation of the Rhineland.

In his autobiography[1] Major-General Sir Kenneth Strong, KBE, CB, writes of his first tour of Germany as a young intelligence officer, which lasted until the end of the occupation, that: 'before then we had been able to witness the beginning of Nazism in Germany. The Rhineland was one of the main centres of activity and propaganda of the emerging Nazi Party and our duties included ensuring that the Nazis did not become a threat to the security of our occupation troops.'

After his release from prison, Hitler began to reorganize his movement. The current fear of communism, embittered feelings of defeat after 1918, widespread unemployment, the collapse of industries, inflation and, eventually, the great depression all drove Germans in the direction of the NSDAP. Moreover, the Treaty of Versailles and the reparations imposed on Germany were regarded as unfair.

The Weimar Republic was at the mercy of a number of parties and none of them had enough of a majority to be able to act decisively. The original, largely political, complexion of Hitler's movement soon gave way to a rather more military stance. His reaction to the occupation was anger: anger that the French had entered the Ruhr; anger that they had tried to separate the Rhineland from Germany and anger that France had used 'coloured troops' among its occupation forces.[2]

Paul Joseph Goebbels,[3] the most intelligent and literate of the Nazi top brass, was born in Rheydt, west of the Rhine near Krefeld, in what was to become the Belgian zone during the Allied occupation. He left school at Easter

1917 and attended Bonn, Freiburg and Heidelberg universities. After working in the Dresdener Bank in Cologne, a friend from his school days introduced him to nationalist and national socialist circles where he took part in meetings and discussions.

In 1924 Franz von Wiegerhaus, the Eberfeld nationalist politician and Prussian diet deputy, appointed Goebbels as his secretary at a time when his duties included speaking at party meetings and editing a small weekly magazine. By the end of the year, Goebbels had become acquainted with prominent national socialists in west Germany.

In 1925 he was appointed manager of the Rheinland-Nord Gau area of the NSDAP. In August 1925 he wrote in his diary that: 'Hitler's book is wonderful. What a political instinct.' It was followed by an entry of 11 September in which he wrote of 'Publication of a fortnightly News Sheet [National Socialist Letters], publisher Stresser, editor Moi. … That will be a monstrous load for me. But that must be borne, for the sake of the cause.'[4]

Later, in October, he commented again on Hitler's book: 'Thrilled to bits. Who is this man? Half plebeian, half God. Really Christ or only John?' Goebbels's diary entries give evidence of his many talks in the north Rhine area. He also comments on political events. For example, on 21 October 1925, he writes that: 'Locarno agreements published. Horrible. How can a modern German statesmen accept these shameful agreements? Stresemann is a perfect rogue. … I spoke 189 times between 1 October 1924 and 1 October 1925. Enough to kill oneself. I look forward to Hitler on Saturday/Sunday.'

The diary entry for 6 November 1925 recounts a meeting

with Hitler that explains future developments in the Nazi Party in terms of the devotion of Hitler's followers: 'He is having his meal. He jumps to his feet, there he is. Shakes my hand like an old friend. And those big blue eyes, like stars. He is glad to see me … I am in heaven.'

The diary entry then goes on to explain how Goebbels spoke for two hours while Hitler was speaking elsewhere, but that Hitler had then joined Goebbels later. 'His big speech has quite finished him. Then he makes another half-hour speech here, full of wit, irony, human sarcasm, seriousness and glowing with passion … that man has got everything to be a king.'

On 16 October 1926, at Hitler's suggestion, party comrade Goebbels was directed to leave the Rhineland to take up an appointment as the leader of the local group, Greater Berlin. Goebbels described how hard he had been working for the movement. On 28 December his diary discloses that he spent 'Every day at work on a comprehensive programme for National Socialism', but it also reveals the 'devastating free-for-all fighting' at a meeting when 'a thousand beer glasses were broken and one hundred and fifty [people were] wounded, two dead'.

Goebbels's adulation for Hitler continues throughout the diary. He spent the day with Hitler in Cologne on 17 June 1929 and comments that: 'He knows everything … [he is] a genius … the day will come when Hitler will lead us out of our misery.' More ecstatic writing came in July when he wrote that 'I am his to the end. My last doubts have disappeared. Germany will live. Heil Hitler!'

Among the Allies, however, the reaction to the obvious growth of the NSDAP was quite the contrary. In his account of his service in the Rhineland, General Strong comments that 'Goebbels was a frequent visitor to the occupied territory and on one occasion after he had described the French as *dreckige Waschlappen* [dirty dishcloths], we arrested him. ... Goering was also a frequent visitor to the Rhineland; we kept a close watch on him and his activities because we knew his speeches invariably led to disorder.'[5]

Some of the NSDAP's illegal activities in the occupied territories have already been described in high commission reports, but fresh developments in military training and in the acquisition of arms were becoming evident. The NSDAP provoked a riot in the French zone in Mainz in May 1928 and many people were injured; on this occasion revolvers were in evidence. A similar brawl occurred on 22 July at the NSDAP's congress in the Palatinate at which shots were fired and 50 people were wounded.

On 12 May 1929 the NSDAP held a huge demonstration at Landsthul, also in the Palatinate, which it called '*Deutscher Tag*' and at which some 1000 national socialists were present in uniform. Violent speeches were made against the occupation and there was much 'encouragement of hatred and a warlike spirit'.[6] As a consequence, the high commission prohibited the next meeting, which was to be held at Neustadt on 28 May. Armed combat with local communists in surrounding towns and villages had become a frequent occurrence, at which firearms were often used and which often resulted in casualties. Nazi Party membership had been calculated to have steadily increased from 100,000 to 150,000 between October 1928 and 1 September 1929.

Paul Tirard, the French high commissioner, wrote that, in his view, the secret societies were threatening both the unoccupied and the occupied territories.[7] He did not feel that the German authorities 'showed much haste in applying their own laws on the demand of the Allied governments'. He reports that during the year 1929 the general officer commanding the British armies of occupation became worried about the activities of the NSDAP – 'who did not hesitate to perform military exercises in uniform in the Wiesbaden Zone' – and so took the matter to the high commission, which in turn forbade all such contraventions.

The German commissioner, Baron Langwerth von Simmern, 'rose vehemently against these orders which he considered violated personal and political liberties'. The high commission responded by suggesting that people's liberties were always respected and that the quarrel against the NSDAP was on account of its military activities, which were against the rules of the Treaty of Versailles.

Monsieur Tirard regarded the *Stahlhelm* (steel helmet), which was a counterrevolutionary veterans' organization, to be as equally dangerous as the NSDAP. As a nationalist organization that contained within its ranks some former soldiers who had undergone military training, it was forbidden in the occupied territories. In January 1929 the French authorities found that a number of young people who were members of the *Stahlhelm* were living in their zone; they were arrested and tried by a military court; two were sentenced to eight days' imprisonment and three were fined.

The *Reitervereine* were also suspect in the occupied zones, for they also, for the greater part, were former cavalry officers who had served in the Kaiser's army.

Intelligence

General Strong comments on the distress, during the years of the Rhineland occupation, at the apparent failure of many of the authorities in London to recognize the growth of the Nazi Party. The War Office had a very small staff working on Germany.

> They were fully occupied studying the many reports about clandestine German rearmament that were reaching us from a variety of sources. Nevertheless, I think that they were much more conscious of the future political dangers than were other authorities in London, although they all, including the War Office, gave the impression of considerable scepticism about the potential importance of Hitler and his Party.
>
> The French also had their difficulties. Even when their military attachés were eventually able to collect indisputable evidence of the expansion of the German Army and Air Force, they found it hard to persuade their superiors in Paris to pay attention to their information.

The British were particularly fortunate in their military attaché at the British embassy in Berlin, Colonel (later Major-General) James Marshall-Cornwall. In a dispatch to the Foreign Office of 13 May 1930, Sir Horace Rumbold, the British ambassador at the time, enclosed a report from his military attaché who had been speaking recently to Colonel Erich Kühlenthal of the *Reichswehr* ministry. According to the latter, the national socialist movement was even 'more of a menace than communism as its principles and theories were entirely destructive; another serious feature of the movement was the ascendancy of its leader Adolf Hitler.' Sir Horace added that the 'strength of this absurd movement seems to lie in Herr Hitler's personality and nothing else'.

In a memorandum dated 8 May 1930, Colonel Marshall-Cornwall wrote of a form of 'mad-dog dictatorship' promoted by the national socialists. His opinion of Hitler was of a 'marvellous orator who possesses an extraordinary gift for hypnotizing his audience and gaining adherents. ... Even though his policy is a negative one, his personal magnetism is such as to win over quite reasonable people to his standard and it is this which constitutes the chief danger of the movement.'[8] In Colonel Marshall-Cornwall's opinion, the heads of a number of young officers had been turned towards the national socialist movement as a means of escape from Germany's financial and political troubles.

The Foreign Office minute that was written in response to these reports reads: 'Yes, the strength of this absurd movement seems to lie in Herr Hitler's personality and nothing else – and he is not even a German national, he is an Austrian.' Within the Foreign Office file for Berlin 1930 lies another document on the industrial mobilization of Germany under the title of *Output of War Material in the*

Future: Concealed Stocks, written by a British military expert in Berlin called Colonel F. W. Gosset, CMG, DSO.[9] The Foreign Office minute records that it had been seen by the Secretary of State and that the Committee of Imperial Defence was in possession of the information.

Harold Nicolson, the first secretary to the British embassy in Berlin under Sir Horace Rumbold, wrote to Sir Orme Sargent at the Foreign Office on 7 August 1929 and expressed the opinion that immediately Allied troops were withdrawn from the Rhineland, Germans would make plans for evading the demilitarized clauses and establish a secret system of defences covering the Ruhr. The majority of German public opinion would support the military authorities and there was no doubt that the French had considerable grounds for apprehension. He called attention to changes of attitude on the part of the German government once evacuation had taken place.

Orme Sargent, writing on 13 August, thought that 'Mr Nicolson is fully justified ... the less said about Rhineland demilitarization for the next few years the better, in the hope that in the interval something may turn up to change the present German outlook.' He continued: 'There is no danger of conscription being restored in open violation of the Treaties, nor need we fear that the German government will defiantly station troops in the demilitarized zone.' Here was another example of official partial sightedness, on the British side, to events in Germany. Recent research has shown it was policy to disregard, for the most part, information coming from that source.[10]

Anthony Clayton, in his *History of the Intelligence Corps*[11] devotes a chapter to what he calls 'The Years of Neglect

1919–1929'. In the search for economies, he maintains that military intelligence soon became an easy target. There was a public and military reaction against any major European commitment. The wartime intelligence corps was run down. 'Intelligence was seen, once again, as ungentlemanly.'

He goes on to describe the small number of intelligence staff in the British Army of the Rhine, and their numbers dwindled as the years of the occupation went by. As already mentioned in the case of Robert Coulson, in 1927, the severely reduced intelligence organization became known as the civil affairs and security branch, which was headed by Lieutenant-Colonel R. W. Oldfield, the superior officer of the young Major-General Sir Kenneth Strong.

Anthony Clayton's contribution to the subject of intelligence in the Rhine army includes the care that was taken to watch the numerous German societies that were trying to conduct clandestine military training under a variety of guises; art, literature, music, nature, aviation, disaster relief, sports and games of all types; religious groups and ex-servicemen. By the end of the decade attention was being focused on the emerging national socialist party.

The memorandum that Lieutenant-Colonel Oldfield submitted on 12 December 1929, on his departure from Germany, reveals both the structure and the methods of intelligence in the British occupied areas.[12] Of particular interest is the employment of agents infiltrated into various communities to provide information. One such was planted into a local branch of the NSDAP in Wiesbaden which was 'to be feared by its open flouting of

12. The British army leaves the Rhineland: 2nd battalion of the Royal Fusiliers marches through Wiesbaden on its way to the railway station, 12 December 1929.

the Ordinance … forbidding training of a military nature in occupied territories'.

The agent was supported by money paid for his

services; he worked himself into a higher position within the NSDAP by means of funds supplied to him.

The sorry part of these intelligence enterprises was that little notice was taken in official circles of the information passed by members of the opposition to Hitler.[13] Perhaps those of the occupation were at fault by having had so little communication with German nationals. But then, few German nationals of consequence were anxious to meet the Allies living in the Rhineland.

Chapter 10

THE PREMATURE EVACUATION OF THE RHINE ARMIES

Once the agreements of the Hague conference had reached Koblenz, the high commission began to prepare for the evacuation of the second zone based there. On 16 September 1929 the high commission met and decided on Wiesbaden as its future location. German uneasiness was increased by the news that an extra 200 French troops would accompany the high commission as a garrison. Official notification was given that the departure from Koblenz, which had begun on 16 September, would be completed by 30 November.

The high commissioners had agreed that Monsieur Tirard alone would attend the ceremony when the French flag was hauled down from the fortress of Ehrenbreitstein at Koblenz on 30 November 1929 to mark the occasion of the second zone having been vacated. The Belgian army would conduct its own ceremony at Aix-la-Chapelle on the evacuation of the Belgian army from the Rhineland. The ceremony at Koblenz took place at 11.15 a.m. and the remainder of the French troops left immediately. A few hours later, Koblenz, Aix-la-Chapelle and other towns of the zone, were bathed in illuminations, torch light processions and expressions of joy. On 30 January 1930 Lord Templemore asked in the House of Lords[1] whether valuable property was being thrown into the Rhine.

The high commission's various national departments were much reduced in the move to Wiesbaden, where it was set up at the Hotel Wilhelma at the northern end of Wilhelmstrasse. The reduction of the British department was greatly in excess of that of any other country, which was a reflection of the Foreign Office's attitude towards the situation in Germany. The three flags of Belgium, Britain and France flew from flagpoles on the roof. A French guard of sentries was perpetually on duty.

During parliamentary questions in the House of Commons on 2 April 1930 Mr Geoffrey Mander, the member of parliament for Wolverhampton, asked the secretary of state for foreign affairs how many British officials remained in occupied territory, where they were working and what duties they were performing.

Mr Hugh Dalton replied that there were only five British officials on the staff of the British section of the Rhineland high commission in Wiesbaden. (The French had 40.) Their duties were to keep in touch with the French authorities and report on the situation. They would be withdrawn on the final evacuation by French troops on 30 June 1930.

13. German citizens watch the ceremony while a German policeman salutes.

On account of the move of the high commission from Koblenz, my father was required to move with it. As a family we exchanged the house and garden at Oberwerth for a large flat in Wiesbaden on the Sonnenberger Strasse, which led to the hilly and wooded area of Sonnenberg. Our governess, Lotte Nieburgh, and our cook, Marlchen, came with us. Afternoon walks were even better than they had been in Koblenz and they included a cave previously used by robbers and a Greek chapel with onion-shaped domes; inside stood the tomb of a princess, with her effigy in white marble lying on the top. To be in new surroundings was much to our taste.

General Thwaites reported on a good deal of activity by the NSDAP in the Wiesbaden area.

On the extreme right of the German political

> parties, is to be found a noisy majority called the NSDAP. Its avowed aims are the cancellation of the Versailles Treaty; the overthrow of the republic and the setting up of a dictator in Germany. The chauvinistic ideals and increasing vocal anti-allied propaganda of its members, gradually rendered them as distasteful to the occupied authorities as they were to the Republic government of their own country. ... In 1929 their attitude became more hostile towards the occupation. The High Commission under pressure from the Headquarters of the British Army of the Rhine, forbade the wearing of the Party uniform in all occupied zones.[2]

This could hardly have been expressed more clearly.

Since the possibility of an early evacuation of the British army had been so much discussed, in order, as he wrote, 'not to be caught unawares', Lieutenant-General Sir William Thwaites set a winter exercise on the evacuation of the British army for the administrative staff to work out in detail, in October 1928. It was completed early in February 1929; on 17 February a mission from the War Office arrived in Wiesbaden to discuss the scheme. In an interview between General Thwaites and the secretary of state for war, when it came to be examined, it was agreed that the exercise could be carried out in three months.

Following The Hague conference in August, at which service members were in attendance, the decision was reached that the evacuation of the British Army of the Rhine should begin on 14 September; the Germans were to waive all claims as from 1 September. Completed arrangements were then put in train for the evacuation of animals, stores, and soldiers' wives and children by several lines of communication: these consisted of Antwerp, Rotterdam, Ostend, and the rail and waterway systems of four nations, namely Germany, France, Belgium and the Netherlands.

Some 300 dogs and cats were transported from the Rhineland, plus the Royal Welsh Fusiliers' goat. Dogs and cats needed to undergo three months' quarantine on arrival in England. The War Office was prepared to write a special letter in respect of the goat, which was sentenced to 28 days of detention at Tidworth, the regiment's home station. By 14 November all the women and children had left Wiesbaden and all the billets had been handed on. General Thwaites reported that the attitude of the German authorities during the last days of the occupation was extremely correct.

The Sarasani Circus had been allotted part of the British army recreation ground in Wiesbaden. One evening a performance was given, without payment, to the remaining members of the British garrison. On arrival, General Thwaites was received by the full staff of the circus who stood awaiting him. The band played the 'general salute' followed by the Royal Artillery slow march (General Thwaites was an artillery man); the audience of several hundred rose to its feet.

A dinner from the French commander-in-chief followed the next day and on 11 December General Thwaites and his staff went to Mainz to take official leave of the French general at the headquarters of his bridgehead. He was received by a French squadron of cavalry on arrival and escorted to the Palais Ducal, the official residence of General Guillaumat, where a guard of honour was drawn up to receive him. On his departure, the French cavalry escorted him over the Mainz bridge, where General Thwaites inspected them, before returning to Wiesbaden. He attended the opera for the last time that evening, with a performance of Wagner's *The Flying Dutchman*, his choice.

Chapter 11
FINAL EVACUATION OF THE ALLIED ARMIES

On the morning of 12 December, General Thwaites made his official visit to the German municipal authorities in Wiesbaden at which Dr Ehrler, the *Regierungspräsident* and all heads of department, totalling 25 people in all, were present. The general made a formal speech in German. He ended with the words, '*Für alle Zukunft, sage ich Ihnen allen, Lebewohl!*'[1] The *Regierungspräsident* made a correct, but friendly reply. He concluded with words to the effect that a warm welcome would always be accorded to members of the British Army of the Rhine should they choose to return to Wiesbaden at any future date.

At 2.00 p.m. the same afternoon, the ceremony of hauling down the Union Jack at British army headquarters at the Hohenzollern Hotel took place.

14. The Union Jack is lowered for the last time at the headquarters of the British Army of the Rhine in Wiesbaden, 12 December 1929. General Thwaites and Mr William Seeds, the British high commissioner, are in the front row.

At exactly 1.55 p.m. the company of Royal Fusiliers (the only remaining soldiers, of which there were approximately 100) with band and colours, formed up opposite the gateway of GHQ.

They were inspected by the commander-in-chief, who then took his stand in front of the line, with his staff behind him. Mr William Seeds, the British high commissioner, stood at his right hand side.

A large number of French officers and their wives watched the ceremony from the windows of the Hohenzollern Hotel. A warning to lower the flag was then given by a long roll of drums; it was slowly hauled down, the troops presenting arms to the regimental colour being lowered.

15. A contingent of French troops salutes as the flags are lowered.

When the flag had been detached from the halyard, General Thwaites presented it to the Royal Fusiliers for safe keeping because the second battalion had been one of the first units to cross the Rhine on 13 December 1918 and, in its second tour of duty, was the last to leave on 12 December 1929, exactly 11 years later. General Thwaites then drove by car to the railway station at Wiesbaden, where he inspected the French third battalion 21st regiment, which was drawn up to give farewell to the departing British troops. The regimental band played the Royal Artillery slow march.

Meanwhile, the Royal Fusiliers, with their band, marched through the streets of Wiesbaden lined by a large number of German inhabitants. Twenty paces away from the assembled French battalion at the railway station, General Guillaumat standing in front of them, the Royal Fusiliers, marching to attention, with bayonets fixed, broke into slow time; the band struck up with the *Marseillaise.*[2] My father, who was standing opposite the French general, saw how moved he was at this unaccustomed gesture, which had never previously been shown to an allied army.

The British army embarked in trains and reached Ostend the next morning. There they were greeted by a Belgian general and the British military attaché in Brussels; a Belgian band played. There was an army welcoming party in Dover. At Victoria station in London, Major-General E. Evans, who was the director of movements and quartering, appeared with some former members of the Rhine army. The Fusiliers marched to Liverpool Street *en route* for Colchester. General Thwaites wrote[3] sadly of his own departure.

> It seemed a suitable ending to what may be said to have been a historic event, namely the completion of evacuation of the Rhineland by British troops, after eleven years of occupation, that the General Officer Commanding was obliged to drive to his private residence in London in a taxi-cab; the loading of his baggage on which was performed by his last remaining troops.

Clearly, the general was hurt by the lack of a last courtesy. Was it memory loss on behalf of a clerk in the War Office, or just another example of a desire to forget the existence of an army on the Rhine? In Wiesbaden the high commission's work continued, protected and surrounded by French troops. But one British soldier, Corporal Hutt of the Military Police, remained behind in a German hospital; he was too ill to move and was not expected to recover. William Seeds, the British high commissioner, wrote to the secretary of state for foreign affairs, Arthur Henderson, on 23 December, to relate the circumstances of Corporal Hutt's funeral; they were remarkable.

By orders of General Guillaumat, a military funeral was provided by the French army; a detachment of French troops fetched the gun carriage with the coffin from the hospital. Colonel Fischer, the senior French officer, with a group of others, followed on foot to the cemetery, a distance of two miles and he remained there while the chaplain of the British church in Wiesbaden read the funeral service. The British high commissioner and members of his staff, with the British consul-general at Frankfurt, attended.

An unexpected feature was the appearance of a detachment of the German police, who had brought a large wreath. The War Office had enabled Corporal Hutt's parents to travel from England. His father, himself a former soldier, was deeply moved by the honours paid to his dead son.

During the month of January 1930 William Seeds was appointed British ambassador in Rio de Janeiro. The duties of British high commissioner devolved upon his political officer, my father James Herbertson, from 30 January for the remainder of the life of the high commission. Monsieur Tirard considered that the appointment, even at such a late stage, should have gone to another ambassador. Clearly the Foreign Office did not think so.

At my father's inauguration at the 388th session of the high commission,[4] Monsieur Tirard decided to put his feelings aside, and spoke amicably enough. '*J'adresse à Monsieur Herbertson, appelé, à suppléer Monsieur William Seeds dans ses fonctions, un cordial salut. Je n'ai pas besoin d'ajouter qu'il peut être certain de mon concours. Depuis de longues années nous avons pu apprécier ses qualités et son esprit de loyauté; nous l'assurons de toute notre amitié.*'

The Belgian high commissioner associated himself with those words. James Herbertson replied in French to which Monsieur Tirard responded with warmth – '*Mon cher ami*' – and complimented my father not only on his sentiments, but on his practical knowledge of the French language.

There followed a hectic five months for my parents. The flag pole in the courtyard of our block of flats began to fly a Union Jack; a smaller version was attached to my father's car.

Guests came to dinner in large numbers for which a chef was employed to help our cook Marlchen, especially for the occasion of the celebration of the official birthday of King George V when General Guillaumat came with his wife. Correspondence with the Foreign Office seems to have hinged largely on the possibility that the French army might not be able to leave the Rhineland by the date prescribed at The Hague, namely 30 June 1930. The topics discussed at the meetings of the high commission included a good deal *'au sujet de la NSDAP'*. On 14 April 1930 it was reported that the NSDAP had 90,000 men of the *Sturmabteilungen.*[5] '(*Ses sections de jeunesses equipées et instruites militariment.*)' I recall my father's anxiety at these developments.

He wrote to Orme Sargent at the Foreign Office on 20 June 1930. 'With regard to the British department, all arrangements have been made for the closing down of the office. Secret documents are being taken by courier to HM Consulate at Cologne; all unnecessary archives have already been destroyed; the combination safe is being dispatched to HM Consulate at Antwerp.'

Eventually, the French evacuation, difficult though it had become, was nearing completion; troop trains began to leave. The last *Séance de la Haute Commission interalliée des Terres rhénans* was held on Saturday 28 June 1930. Paul Tirard spoke first and began, *'Messieurs. La Haute Commission a achevé sa tâche.'*[6]

He thanked his allied colleagues for the cooperation and trust they had shown for 12 years. Each one had done his duty to his country. 'We have tried in this country to follow a policy [that is] both just and humane.'

16. The author and her sister with the flag pole flying the Union Jack in the garden of their home in Wiesbaden, spring 1929.

Monsieur Le Jeune de Münsbach, the high commissioner for Belgium spoke next. He acknowledged his melancholy because this was to be the last time that they were to meet together.

My father, James Herbertson, spoke last on behalf of Great Britain. He said he wished to express the profound appreciation of the British department for the courtesy continually shown in its regard and the constant help that had been given in the course of the passing years. He referred to 'the very difficult periods' the high commission had experienced; it had been largely through the president that they had been surmounted with success.

The German commissioner, Baron Langwerth von Simmern, was invited to join the proceedings. He then also made a valedictory speech. He expressed the view that 30 June 1930, which would see the departure of the occupying forces four-and-a-half years before the date originally set, would mark the beginning of complete and definitive reconciliation between peoples. He wished to assure the high commissioners that he would continue to work personally for such *rapprochement*. He invited the high commissioners and their staff to dinner that evening.

On the afternoon of 28 June the three high commissioners, with the French commander-in-chief, visited the French and German military cemeteries at Mainz and the British and German military cemetery at Wiesbaden. They laid wreaths in memory of those who were buried there. The German commissioner accompanied them at these ceremonies.

Finally, at 9.30 a.m. on 30 June 1930, the Belgian, British and French flags were lowered from the roof of the Wilhelma Hotel, the seat of the high commission, in the presence of the three high commissioners, General

Guillaumat, and some French officers, who all stood at the front of the building. A small detachment of French soldiers stood nearby. All presented arms as the flags came down and the appropriate national anthem was played. My sister and I, with our mother, had a place from which to watch, opposite the headquarters. The flags were given to the appropriate high commissioner.

Paul Tirard, with General Guillaumat, made for Mainz, the headquarters of the French Army of the Rhine, and has left in his *La France sur le Rhin* an account of the ceremonies that marked the departure of the French army from the Rhineland. Coming down a flight of steps, then across a small square at 11.30 a.m., Monsieur Tirard and the general stopped to face a parade of troops. The general drew his sword in honour of the flags of France; then came a command 'salute to the colours'. The last French flag in the Rhineland was lowered slowly on the roof of the Palais Grand-Ducal. Tirard reflected on the generals who had lived there during the past ten years and spoke about how Marshals Joffre, Fayolle and Foch had worked there. An NCO carried the flag in due solemnity in front of the troops who marched to the railway station, with the band and colonel marching before them. Monsieur Tirard followed by car and entered the train last of all. France had left the Rhine.

Just before 3.00 p.m. my father, my mother, my sister and I drove to the railway station at Wiesbaden. The chaplain at the English church of St Augustine of Canterbury, where my father had read the lessons, was there to bid us farewell. My father had sent a telegram to the Foreign Office. It read 'EVACUATION COMPLETED'. As he

17. Final act of the occupation, 30 June 1930. The three high commissioners of France, Belgium and Great Britain at the headquarters of the IARHC in Wiesbaden, as the allied flags are lowered and national anthems played.

entered the train, he became the last allied official to leave the formerly occupied territory.

La haute commission a achevé sa tâche

Whether Monsieur Tirard meant that their task had been achieved, or concluded, is not clear, but with hindsight it would appear that neither was the case. In his book he wrote:

> After the departure of our troops, the Rhineland was invaded by the hordes of Hitler's soldiers and the division *Stahlhelm,* serious troubles, looting in the towns, were a political revenge. The German

> authorities had failed to encourage the population to be calm and dignified and allowed a situation to develop which swiftly got out of hand. ... The immediate results of our departure, the violent incidents which were a result of bands of terrorists coming from the right bank, showed the double face of Germany, alternately turning first to the Right and then to the Left, towards peace and then towards war.[7]

In the midst of a severe economic depression, Germany failed to provide a strong and stable democratic government once independence from occupation had been reached. It had been a serious mistake on the part of the occupying powers to have withdrawn their armies before having made sure that the disarmament clauses of the Treaty of Versailles had been met. The people on the ground were clearly in the best position to measure and report on what progress had been made towards honouring these clauses.

Stresemann's papers provide evidence of the civil government's collaboration with the military in freeing the *Reichswehr* from the supervision of the Allies, and making possible Germany's massive renewal of military power.[8] Opponents to the Nazi regime within Germany were unflagging in sending signals about what might lie ahead. In the British case, Patricia Meehan[9] comments on the absence of a political intelligence department at the Foreign Office that could collate and analyse information coming out of Germany on anti-Nazi activities.

To cut short the occupation, to miss what its continued

existence might secure, appeared to be official policy. It was a dangerous one; the Nazi Party made steady progress and sprang into the vacuum caused by the weakness of the Weimar Republic: it gained 107 seats in the *Reichstag* on 14 September 1930; in the 1932 election the Nazis achieved nearly 14 million votes. On 30 January 1933 Hitler became chancellor of Germany and, in 1934, he was made leader and commander-in-chief. Two years later, defying the demilitarized zone, his soldiers became the next occupiers of the Rhineland. The Second World War was only three years away.

NOTES

Introduction

1. Sir Herbert Plumer (1857–1932).
2. General Sir Charles Harington, *Plumer of Messines*, London: John Murray, 1935.
3. James Herbertson, LVO, OBE (1883–1974).
4. General Sir Kenneth Strong, *Intelligence at the Top*, London: Cassell, 1968.
5. Margaret Pawley, *In Obedience to Instructions*, Barnsley: Pen & Sword, 1999.
6. Alan Bullock, *Hitler and Stalin: Parallel Lives*, London: Harper Collins, 1991, p. 570.
7. Earl of Avon, *The Eden Memoirs: Facing the Dictators*, London: Cassell, 1962.

Chapter 1: Civil Affairs (1918–20)

1. Frederich Ebert was a former saddle-maker who died on 26 February 1925.
2. Field Marshal von Hindenburg (1847–1934) was a Prussian career soldier who became a national hero after his success on the eastern front (1914–16). He was brought out of his retirement in 1926 to become president of Germany.

3. General Erich Ludendorf (1856–1937) was quarter-master general of the German Second Army (1914) and later served under Hindenburg.
4. Georges Clemenceau (1841–1929) was the son of a doctor and he too trained as such. Leader of the Radical Party; minister of the interior (1906); premier and minister of war (1917) at age of 76; he served until 1920.
5. From papers at the Imperial War Museum.
6. Preface to Keith Nelson, *Victors Divided: America and the Allies in Germany, 1918–1923,* Berkeley: University of California Press, 1975.
7. Ibid.
8. B. H. Liddell-Hart, *Foch, the Man of Orleans 1914–1924,* Harmondsworth: Penguin, 1937, vol II, p 431.
9. Preface, *Victors Divided.*
10. Pierrepont B. Noyes, *A Goodly Heritage,* New York: Rinehart, 1958.
11. Ibid., p. 249 has the text in full.
12. Ibid.
13. Walter A. McDougall, *France's Rhineland Diplomacy, 1914–1924: The Last Bid for a Balance of Power in Europe,* Princeton, NJ: Princeton University Press, 1978.
14. Sidney Waterlow was a British diplomat.
15. Noyes, *A Goodly Heritage,* p. 260.
16. Ibid. p. 250.

Chapter 2: Military Affairs (1918–22)

1. Harington, *Plumer of Messines.*
2. The original letter is housed in the Imperial War Museum.
3. Ibid.
4. General Sir William Robertson, *From Private to Field Marshal,* London: Constable, 1921.
5. General John Joseph Pershing was commander in chief of the American Expeditionary Force.
6. Nelson, *Victors Divided,* p. 31.
7. Alfred E. Cornebise, *The Amaroc News: The Daily Newspaper*

of the American Forces in Germany 1919–1923*, Carbondale: Southern Illinois University Press, 1981.

8. Heath Twitchell Jr, *Allen: The Biography of an Army Officer, 1859–1930*, New Brunswick: Rutgers University Press, 1974.
9. Major General H. T. Allen, *The Rhineland Occupation*, Indianapolis: Bobbs-Merrill Company, 1927; and Major General H. T. Allen, *My Rhineland Journal*, London: Hutchinson, 1924.
10. Nelson, *Victors Divided.*
11. Ibid., p.39.
12. Ibid., p. 23.
13. McDougall, *France's Rhineland Diplomacy*, p. 153.
14. Noyes, *A Goodly Heritage*. p. 252.
15. The *Frei Corps* were volunteer soldiers.
16. Literally 'sharpshooters'.
17. The new German army.
18. FO 371/9844.
19. Tirard, *La France sur le Rhin*, Paris: Plon, 1930.
20. These noble words were refuted somewhat in two examples in documents written by Tirard in 1918 and 1919 (and deposited in Paris) suggesting that 'economics were the key to French influence on the Rhine'. See McDougall, *France's Rhineland Diplomacy*, p. 44.
21. Ferdinand Tuohy, *Occupation: 1918–1930: A Postscript to the Western Front*, London: Thornton Butterworth, 1931.
22. Ibid., p. 84.
23. General Charles Mangin (1866–1925); he trained in colonial warfare and had the highest regard for African troops.
24. Appendices, Allen, *The Rhineland Occupation*.

Chapter 3: Separatism in the Rhineland (1918–24)

1. McDougall, *France's Rhineland Diplomacy*, p. 47.
2. Adam Dorten, *The Rhenish Republic: Its Tendencies and History*, Wiesbaden, 1919, p. 15.
3. G. E. R. Gedye, *The Revolver Republic*, London: Arrowsmith, 1930.

4. Charles Williams, *Adenauer: The Father of the New Germany*, Boston, MA: Little, Brown & Company, 2000, p. 48.
5. McDougall, *France's Rhineland Diplomacy*, p. 48.
6. Tuohy, *Occupation*, p. 171.
7. Ibid.
8. Nelson, *Victors Divided*, p. 111.
9. David Williamson, *The British in Germany: 1918–1930*, Oxford: Berg, 1991, p. 44.
10. Harry E. Nadler, *Rhenish Separatist Movements during the Early Weimar Republic: 1918–1924*, New York: Garland Publishing Inc., 1987.
11. Dorten, *The Rhenish Republic*.
12. FO 371/9844.
13. Ibid.
14. Lord Kilmarnock (1876–1928). Third, second and first secretaries to various embassies (1900–19), chargé d'affaires, Berlin (1920).
15. FO 371/10756.
16. Ruth Henig, *The Weimar Republic: 1919–1933*, London: Routledge, 1998, p. 25.
17. FO 371/12130, pp. 76–7.
18. Ibid.

Chapter 4: American Forces Leave the Rhine (1922–23)

1. Nelson, *Victors Divided*, p. 2.
2. Ibid. p. 22.
3. Allen, *The Rhineland Occupation*, p. 170.
4. Twichell, *Allen: The Biography of an Army Officer*, p. 2.
5. Ibid. p.214.
6. Nelson, *Victors Divided*, p. 239.
7. Allen, *My Rhineland Journal*, p. 335.
8. Allen, *The Rhineland Occupation*, p. 251.
9. Nelson, *Victors Divided*, p. 246.
10. Allen, *My Rhineland Journal*, p. 538.

11. FO 371/12130.
12. Tirard, *La France sur le Rhin,* pp. 489–90.

Chapter 5: French and Belgian Troops Enter the Ruhr

1. David Carlton, *Henderson versus MacDonald: The Foreign Policy of the Second Labour Government*, London: Macmillan, 1970, p. 135.
2. Tuohy, *Occupation,* p. 186.
3. FO 371/12130, p. 2.
4. Tuohy, *Occupation,* p. 189.
5. FO 371/12130, p. 11.
6. James Edmonds, *The Occupation of the Rhineland: 1918–1929,* London: HMSO, 1987, p. 249.
7. Ibid., p. 253.
8. FO 371/12130, p. 2.
9. *Dictionary of National Biography* entry.
10. Jonathan Wright, *Gustav Stresemann: Weimar's Greatest Statesman*, Oxford: Oxford University Press, 2002, p. 64.
11. Adolf Hitler, *Mein Kampf,* translated by Ralph Mannheim, London : Hutchinson, 1992.
12. Ibid., pp. 502–3.
13. Ibid.

Chapter 6: Disarmament, Reparations and Locarno (1924–26)

1. John W. Wheeler-Bennett and Hugh Latimer, *Information on the Reparations Settlement,* London: George Allen & Unwin Ltd, 1930, p. 28.
2. This conference was set up in Paris in 1920 and it consisted of the ambassadors of the USA, Britain, Italy and Japan, as well as a French representative.
3. J. Jacobson, *Locarno Diplomacy: Germany and the West, 1925–1929,* Princeton: Princeton University Press, 1972.
4. Lord D'Abernon, *Ambassador of Peace,* London: Hodder &

Stoughton, 1929, vol. 1, pp. 4–5.
5. Wheeler-Bennett and Latimer, *Information on the Reparations Settlement*, p. 55.
6. Ibid., p. 60.
7. Jacobson, *Locarno Diplomacy*, p. 8.
8. FO 371/13640, p. 34.

Chapter 7: The British Army Leaves Cologne for Wiesbaden (1926–29)

1. FO 371/13640.
2. Apex, *The Uneasy Triangle*, London: Murray, 1931, pp. 230–2.
3. General Sir William Robertson, *From Private to Field Marshal*.
4. General Sir Alexander Godley, *Life of an Irish Soldier*, London: John Murray, 1939.
5. James Edmonds, *The Occupation of the Rhineland: 1918–1929*, p. 264.
6. Lieutenant-General Sir John Du Cane served in South Africa from 1899 to 1902; he commanded the 15th corps from 1916 to 1918; was a British representative with Marshal Foch in 1918; and was master–general of munitions from 1923 to 1924.
7. FO 371/13640, p. 17.
8. Williams, *Adenauer*, p. 166.
9. Ibid., p. 168.
10. FO 371/13640, p. 4.
11. Edmonds, *The Occupation of the Rhineland*, p. 286.
12. WO 106/463.
13. FO 371/14375, p. 9.

Chapter 8: The Inter-Allied Rhineland High Commission

1. Maie Casey, *Tides and Eddies*, London: Michael Joseph, 1966.
2. In 1926 she married Richard Gardiner Casey KG, PC, CH,

DSO, MC, later governor-general of Australia from 1965 to 1969; Minister of state, resident in the Middle East and member of the War Cabinet from 1942 to 1943; and governor of Bengal from 1944 to 1946.

3. Translated as 'Victorious we shall beat France'.
4. Tirard, *La France sur le Rhin,* p. 184. What follows is a rough translation from the French.
5. FO 371/13640, p. 13.
6. WO 106/463.
7. FO 371/14375.
8. Ibid.
9. D'Abernon, *Ambassador of Peace* (diary of Lord D'Abernon), vol 3, p. 10.
10. Ibid., p. 19.
11. James Lees-Milne, *Harold Nicolson: A Biography,* vol. 1, 1886–1929, London: Chatto & Windus, 1980, p. 333.

Chapter 9: The Development of Nationalistic Societies (1929–30)

1. Strong, *Intelligence at the Top.*
2. As shown in Hitler's book *Mein Kampf,* which he dictated while he was in prison, p. 295.
3. Paul Joseph Goebbels 1897–1945.
4. Helmut Heiber (ed.) *The Early Goebbels Diaries, 1925–1926,* London: Weidenfeld & Nicolson, 1962, p. 31.
5. Strong, *Intelligence at the Top.*
6. FO 371/14375, p. 3.
7. Tirard, *La France sur le Rhin.*
8. FO 371/14362.
9. Ibid.
10. Patricia Meehan, *The Unnecessary War: Whitehall and the German Resistance to Hitler,* London: Sinclair-Stevenson, 1992.
11. Anthony Clayton, *Forearmed: A History of the Intelligence Corps,* London: Brassey's (UK), 1993.

12. *On the Work of the Section of Civil Affairs and Security, British Army of the Rhine*, Intelligence Corps Museum.
13. Meehan, *The Unnecessary War*.

Chapter 10: The Premature Evacuation of the Rhine Armies

1. FO 371/14354.
2. WO 106/463.

Chapter 11: Final Evacuation of the Allied Armies

1. 'For the future, I wish you all, farewell.'
2. WO 106/463.
3. Ibid.
4. From then onwards all meetings of the high commission were conducted in French, as were all the subsequent reports.
5. FO 371/14354.
6. 'The high commission has completed (or achieved) its task.'
7. Tirard, *La France sur le Rhin*, pp. 444–6.
8. See Introduction in Hans W. Gatzke, *Stresemann and the Rearmament of Germany*, New York: W. W. Norton & Company Inc., 1969.
9. Meehan, *The Unnecessary War*.

REFERENCES

Foreign Office Documents

FO 371/9844
FO 371/10756
FO 371/12130
FO 371/13640
FO 371/14354
FO 371/14375
FO 371/14362

War Office Documents

WO 106/463

Allen, Major General H. T., *My Rhineland Journal*, London: Hutchinson, 1924.

The Rhineland Occupation, Indianapolis: Bobbs Merrill Co., 1927.

Apex (Robert Coulson), *The Uneasy Triangle*, London: Murray, 1931.

Avon, Earl of, *The Eden Memoirs: Facing the Dictators*, London: Cassell, 1962.

Bullock, Alan, *Hitler and Stalin: Parallel Lives*, London: Harper Collins, 1991.

Carlton, David, *Henderson versus MacDonald: The Foreign Policy of the Second Labour Government*, London: Macmillan, 1970.

Casey, Maie, *Tides and Eddies*, London: Michael Joseph, 1966.

Clayton, Anthony, *Forearmed: A History of the Intelligence Corps*, London: Brassey's (UK), 1993.

Cornebise, Alfred E., *The Amaroc News: The Daily Newspaper of the American Forces in Germany, 1919–1923*, Carbondale: Southern Illinois University Press, 1981.

D'Abernon, Lord, *Ambassador of Peace*, 3 vols, London: Hodder & Stoughton, 1929–32.

Dorten, Adam, *The Rhenish Republic: Its Tendencies and History*, Wiesbaden, 1919.

Edmonds, James, *The Occupation of the Rhineland, 1918–1929*, London: Her Majesty's Stationery Office, 1987.

Gatzke, Hans W., *Stresemann and the Rearmament of Germany*, New York: W. W. Norton & Company Inc., 1969.

Gedye, G. E. R., *The Revolver Republic*, London: Arrowsmith, 1930.

Godley, General Sir Alexander, *Life of an Irish Soldier*, London: John Murray, 1939.

Harington, General Sir Charles, *Plumer of Messines*, London: John Murray, 1935.

Heiber, Helmut (ed.) *The Early Goebbels Diaries, 1925–1926*, London: Weidenfeld & Nicolson, 1962.

Henig, Ruth, *The Weimar Republic, 1919–1933*, London: Routledge, 1998.

Hitler, Adolf, *Mein Kampf*, translated by Ralph Mannheim, London: Hutchinson, 1992.

Jacobson, J., *Locarno Diplomacy: Germany and the West, 1925–1929*, Princeton, NJ: Princeton University Press, 1972.

Lees-Milne, James, *Harold Nicolson: A Biography*, 2 vols, London: Chatto & Windus, 1980.

Liddell-Hart, B. H., *Foch, the Man of Orleans, 1914–1924*, Harmondsworth: Penguin, 1937.

McDougall, Walter A., *France's Rhineland Diplomacy, 1914–1924: The Last Bid for a Balance of Power in Europe*, Princeton, NJ: Princeton University Press, 1978.

Meehan, Patricia, *The Unnecessary War: Whitehall and the Resistance to Hitler*, London: Sinclair-Stevenson, 1992.

Nadler, Henry E., *Rhenish Separatist Movements during the Early Weimar Republic, 1918–1924*, New York: Garland Publishing Inc, 1987.

Nelson, Keith, *Victors Divided: America and the Allies in Germany, 1918–1923*, Berkeley: University of California Press, 1975.

Noyes, Pierrepont, *A Goodly Heritage*, New York: Rinehart, 1958.

Pawley, Margaret, *In Obedience to Instructions*, Barnsley: Pen & Sword, 1999.

Robertson, General Sir William, *From Private to Field Marshal*, London: Constable, 1921.

Strong, General Sir Kenneth, *Intelligence at the Top: Recollections of an Intelligence Officer*, London: Cassell, 1968.

Tirard, Paul, *La France sur le Rhin*, Paris: Plon, 1930.

Tuohy, F., *Occupation: 1918–1930: A Postscript to the Western Front*, London: Thornton Butterworth, 1931.

Twichell, Heath, Jr, *Allen: The Biography of an Army Officer, 1859–1930*, New Brunswick: Rutgers University Press, 1974.

Wheeler-Bennett, John and Hugh Latimer, *Information on the Reparations Settlement*, London: George Allen & Unwin Ltd, 1930.

Williams, Charles, *Adenauer: The Father of the New Germany*, Boston, MA: Little, Brown & Company, 2000.

Williamson, David, *The British in Germany, 1918–1930*, Oxford: Berg, 1991.

Wright, Jonathan, *Gustav Stresemann: Weimar's Greatest Statesman*, Oxford: Oxford University Press, 2002.

APPENDIX

C.R. B.A.R. No. M.H./45 (BAS).

From: The General Officer Commanding-in-Chief,
BRITISH ARMY OF THE RHINE.

To: The Under Secretary of State,
THE WAR OFFICE, LONDON, S.W.I

Mill Hill,
N.W.7.
19th December, 1929.

Sir,

I have the honour to report the following events which took place from the 11th to the 13th December, in case the Army Council should deem it expedient to thank the Governments concerned.

On the 11th December, at 10.35 a.m., accompanied by three staff officers and my

A.D.C., I proceeded by car from Wiesbaden to Mainz to pay an official visit on General Guillaumat, the General Officer Commanding-in-Chief, Allied Armies of Occupation, in order to say "good-bye" to him. On reaching the precincts of the bridge over the Rhine at Mainz, a French Squadron of Cavalry met me, and escorted me to the "Palais Ducal", the official residence of General Guillaumat. I was received there by a guard of honour, consisting of a French battalion, which remained in position until I departed. On my departure, the French Cavalry Squadron escorted me over the Mainz Bridge, where they formed up, and I stopped and inspected them before returning to Wiesbaden.

On December 12th, at 11 a.m., accompanied by three staff officers and my A.D.C., I went to the office of the Regierungs President in Wiesbaden, in order to say "good-bye" to the principal German authorities who had been associated in work with the British Army of Occupation. I made them an address in German, and this was replied to by the Regierungs President. He concluded his address with words to the effect that a warm welcome would always be accorded to members of the British Army of the Rhine who might elect to return to Wiesbaden at any future date.

APPENDIX

The ceremony for hauling down the two Union Jacks at General Headquarters was a purely British ceremony, and took place at 2.15 p.m. The orders for this ceremony are attached (marked "A"), also a copy of the notes forwarded to the French (marked "B"), who had expressed the desire to pay a military tribute at the Station to the departing British troops. The ceremony was excellently carried out by the detachment of the Royal Fusiliers, whose dignified bearing impressed the thousands of spectators, British, French and German, that were present.

On conclusion of the ceremony I got into my car and drove to the entrance to the station where, in company with the General Officer Commanding-in-Chief, French Army, I inspected the French Battalion drawn up there.

The detachment of the Royal Fusiliers, after marching a short distance in slow time, and still marching to attention with bayonets fixed, broke into quick time until they arrived 20 paces distant from the French battalion near the Station. From this point they marched past the French battalion, who were "at the present", in slow time to the "Marseillaise", played by the band and drums of the Royal Fusiliers.

They then entered the Station and entrained.

At the Imperial waiting room at the Station, General Guillaumat and a large number, consisting of British officials and French officers, with their wives, assembled to say "good-bye".

The train left Wiesbaden on time, and before reaching Bingen the weather broke, and heavy rain fell.

On arrival at Kreuznach, a final tribute to the British Army was paid by a French battalion drawn up on the platform of the Station.

I had been informed by a letter from the British Military Attache at Brussels (copy attached marked "C"), that General de Callatay, representing the Belgian Minister of Defence, with several Belgian officers of the Ostend garrison and the band, would be at Ostend to pay a compliment to the British Army.

Accordingly, at 10.20 a.m., General Callatay and Staff, accompanied by Lieutenant-Colonel Daubeny, British Military Attache at Brussels, arrived at Ostend, and was received by me and my Staff on board the boat which had been selected by the Belgian Marine to convey me and the remainder of the troops under my command across the channel to Dover. General Callatay made a short address, and referred to the British Army in complimentary terms, to which I made a suitable reply. The Director of Belgian Marine was also present on board, and he had done all in his power for the comfort of myself and my troops. The Belgian band, in the meantime, played suitable music, and had taken the trouble to select some old English airs such as "Tipperary", "When the boys come marching home", etc.

On the quay were some eight members of the British Legion who had come there to take part in the "send-off" of the last troops of the British Army of Occupation.

As the boat slowly moved from the quay, the band played "God save the King". The whole ceremony was awe-inspiring and impressive.

At Dover we were met by Brigadier Sir Hereward Wake, C.M.G., D.S.O., commanding the 12th Infantry Brigade, accompanied by his Brigade Major. Here we said "good-bye".

The Boat Train arrived at Victoria at 5.14 p.m. where we were met by Major-

General E. Evans, C.B., C.M.G., D.S.O., Director of Movements and Quartering, and several members of the Rhine Army. After collecting my baggage I drove away in a taxi-cab to my residence in Kensington.

I have the honour to be,
Sir,
Your obedient Servant,

(sgd). Wm. THWAITES.

LIEUT-GENERAL,
Commanding-in-Chief,
BRITISH ARMY OF THE RHINE.

"A".

INSTRUCTIONS FOR THE FINAL BRITISH CEREMONY
FOR THE LOWERING OF THE UNION JACK.

O-O-O-O-O-O-O-O-O-O-O-O-O-O

1. The ceremony will take place outside General Headquarters on 12th December, 1929, at 14.00 hours.

2. The detachment to take part in the ceremony will be furnished by the 2nd Bn. The Royal Fusiliers, and will consist of one company, strength 2 officers (one Major or Captain and one Lieutenant) and 50 files (excluding supernumeries, Band, Drums and Colours. Dress - Marching Order. A Warrant Officer and a Non-Commissioned Officer in walking out dress, who are to lower the flags, will report to the Garrison Adjutant at G.H.Q. Guard Room at 13.45 hours.

3. The detachment will march to the forming up place as laid down for Ceremonial Guard Mounting, and will be halted when the centre of the Company is opposite the flag at the main entrance to General Headquarters. The Company will then be turned to its front and Officers and Colours will take post as under: -

The Commander three paces in front of the second file from title right, the Lieutenant three paces in front of the second file from the left, and the two officers with the Colours three paces in front of the centre.

In the meantime the Band and Drums will form up on the left of the Company facing in the same direction.

The Company Commander will then open ranks.

On the arrival of the detachment, the old guard will turn out inside the railings in their normal place, all sentries falling in with the Guard. The old Guard will now act on the Detachment Commander's word of command and conform with the movements of the Company.

4. The Officer Commanding, 2nd Bn. The Royal fusiliers, will be attached to the staff of the G.O.C-in-C.

5. At I4.OO hours the General Officer Commanding- in-Chief, accompanied, by his staff, will arrive from the main entrance of General Headquarters, and will be received with a "General Salute"

6. The General Officer Commanding-in-Chief accompanied by his Staff will then inspect the detachment, the Band playing the R.A. Slow March.

7. The General Officer Commanding-in Chief and his Staff will then take up a position in front of the Colours.

8. The Warrant Officer and Non-Commissioned Officer detailed for the purpose will prepare to lower the flags.
9. A long roll will be sounded on the drums, at title conclusion of which the order "Royal Salute" will be given. The Troops will "Present Arms" (the King's Colours and Regimental Colour being lowered) and the flags will be hauled down very slowly during which time the National Anthem will be played.
IO. A second long roll on the drums will then be sounded while the Warrant Officer and the Non-Commissioned Officer remove the flags from the halyards and roll them up.
II. As soon as the G.O.G-in-C and Staff have moved off the detachment will march away in fours with bayonets fixed in slow time until the head of the Drums reaches the Kurhaus Platz when it will break into quick time, and wheel to the left past the Opera House and thence via the Wilhelm Strasse to the Main Station.

The W.O. and N.C.O. with the flags will march abreast five paces in the rear of the band: the Detachment Commander will be five paces in rear of this W.O. and N.C.O.

The old guard will follow 10 paces in rear of the detachment.

I2. The battalion sent by the French Army for the final departure of the British Army will be formed up at the approach to the station. The British detachment will be ordered to break into "slow time" twenty paces before reaching them, and to give "Eyes Right" as it passes, and to break into quick time when its rear is ten paces clear of the French troops.

INDEX

INDEX

INDEX

INDEX

INDEX